THE
EVERYTHING®
MOTHER OF
THE BRIDE
BOOK

A survival guide for Mom!

Shelly Hagen

Adams Media
Avon, Massachusetts

For my mom, who really taught me
how to pull off a dream wedding.

An Everything® Series Book.
Everything® and everything.com are registered trademarks of
F+W Publications, Inc.

Published by Adams Media, an F+W Publications Company
57 Littlefield Street, Avon, MA 02322 U.S.A.
www.adamsmedia.com

ISBN 13: 978-1-59337-246-0
ISBN 10: 1-59337-246-9

Printed in Canada.
J I H G F

Library of Congress Cataloging-in-Publication Data
Hagen, Shelly.
The everything mother of the bride book / Shelly Hagen.
p.   cm.
ISBN 1-59337-246-9
1. Weddings–Planning. 2. Wedding etiquette. 3. Mothers and daughters.
4. Brides–Family relationships. I. Title. II. Series: Everything series.

HQ745.H185 2004
395.2'2–dc22

2004018841

This publication is designed to provide accurate and authoritative information
with regard to the subject matter covered. It is sold with the understanding that
the publisher is not engaged in rendering legal, accounting, or other professional
advice. If legal advice or other expert assistance is required, the services of a
competent professional person should be sought.
—From a *Declaration of Principles* jointly adopted by a Committee of the
American Bar Association and a Committee of Publishers and Associations

Many of the designations used by manufacturers and sellers to distinguish their
products are claimed as trademarks. Where those designations appear in this
book and Adams Media was aware of a trademark claim, the designations have
been printed with initial capital letters.

This book is available at quantity discounts for bulk purchases.
For information, call 1-800-289-0963.

Welcome to the EVERYTHING® series!

THESE HANDY, accessible books give you all you need to tackle a difficult project, gain a new hobby, comprehend a fascinating topic, prepare for an exam, or even brush up on something you learned back in school but have since forgotten.

You can read an *EVERYTHING*® book from cover to cover or just pick out the information you want from our four useful boxes: e-facts, e-ssentials, e-alerts, and e-questions. We literally give you everything you need to know on the subject, but throw in a lot of fun stuff along the way, too.

We now have well over 300 *EVERYTHING*® books in print, spanning such wide-ranging topics as weddings, pregnancy, wine, learning guitar, one-pot cooking, managing people, and so much more. When you're done reading them all, you can finally say you know *EVERYTHING*®!

ⓔ FACTS: Important sound bytes of information

ⓔ ESSENTIALS: Quick and handy tips

ⓔ ALERTS!: Urgent warnings

ⓔ QUESTIONS: Solutions to common problems

THE
EVERYTHING
Series

Dear Reader:

My sister lives in another state, so when she got engaged, my mother dragged *me* around to receptions in progress to check out the food, the band, the atmosphere. ("Blend in," she would say, and then, in a slightly panicked tone, "You're not blending!") We would slide into ceremonies where total strangers were tying the knot and later critique everything, from the soloist and the bridesmaid dresses to the readings and vows.

Meanwhile, I had the unique experience of having two weddings (with the same man, mind you)—an elopement and a traditional ceremony and reception. I didn't plan much for my elopement, but my mom and I spent months planning the big wedding together. I wouldn't trade that time we had for anything in the world—it brought us closer together than we had been in years. We were both busy, but we *had* to sit down and talk—and laugh . . . and *reconnect*.

There are some things a girl—no matter her age, no matter her level of independence—really needs her mom for, and planning a wedding is one of those things. It's a win-win situation: She gets the help she needs planning her big day and you get to be a huge part of it—and it's something she'll never forget.

Shelly Hagen

THE

EVERYTHING

Series

EDITORIAL

Publishing Director: Gary M. Krebs
Managing Editor: Kate McBride
Copy Chief: Laura MacLaughlin
Acquisitions Editor: Kate Burgo
Development Editor: Christina MacDonald
Production Editors: Bridget Brace, Jamie Wielgus

PRODUCTION

Production Director: Susan Beale
Production Manager: Michelle Roy Kelly
Series Designer: Daria Perreault
Cover Design: Paul Beatrice, Matt LeBlanc
Layout and Graphics: Colleen Cunningham,
Rachael Eiben, Michelle Roy Kelly,
John Paulhus, Daria Perreault, Erin Ring

Visit the entire Everything® series at www.everything.com

Contents

Acknowledgments

Thanks to Jessica Faust, my agent at Bookends, for her advice and insight on this book. I also want to thank Helen Edelman, who provided me with invaluable resources for this project. Lastly, I owe a debt of gratitude to the former and current MOBs who gave me their opinions on everything from finding the perfect dress to planning an appropriate budget.

The Top Ten Things an MOB Thinks She'll Never Say—But Does

1. "Yes, Honey, that bustle makes your rear end look huge."

2. "We cannot have a cash bar at the reception."

3. "My ex-husband and I can certainly tolerate each other for *one* day."

4. "Who wants to crash a reception with me to check out the band?"

5. "Well, if it were *my* wedding, I would do it *this* way."

6. "No, Dear, you and your new husband can't live with me after the wedding. Newlyweds need their own space."

7. "Why did you pick *these* dishes for your registry?"

8. "Oh, it's only money, and my daughter's only getting married this one time."

9. "Wow, it might be kind of nice when life returns to normal . . ."

10. "We could not have done one more thing to better prepare ourselves for this wedding. We're *ready*."

Introduction

Well, she did it. Your daughter looked high and low and actually found the perfect man, and he, in turn, gave her a ring to make it official. You're all engaged! (Or at least that's how you feel!) Congratulations! Now what?

Mothers of the bride usually play a huge role in planning the wedding. Your daughter will most likely turn to you as her number one resource for helping her design the wedding of her dreams. Whether you're an old hand at planning parties or you hate the very idea of getting organized and making call after call after call, chances are, you're going to end up doing at least some of the work, and the sooner you get started, the better.

First things first; you'll need to know what the traditional expenses are for your family, as well as for the groom's family, and *then* you'll need to know whether the groom's family plans on breaking with tradition by contributing a significant amount of cash. If so, you'll *all* need to sit down to work out a budget. Take a look at the people sitting across the table from you, because if you're planning this shindig together, you're going to find yourselves in this very same spot sooner than you think, when you need to come up with a guest list and a seating arrangement for the reception.

But let's set aside finances for a moment and take *another* look at the groom's family, because during the pre-wedding months, you're going to be running into your daughter's future in-laws at various parties and planning sessions. If you love them, all of this is going to be really enjoyable. If you can't stand them, you need to find a way to tolerate their idiosyncrasies until the wedding is over.

What are your duties as MOB? Basically, to assist the bride in the planning of the wedding. Beware: That one little sentence belies the fact that there are many, many issues to deal with when planning a wedding—vendors to interview, a budget to work with, bridesmaids running roughshod all over the bride, in-laws who may not see eye to eye with your daughter, and last but not least, the demands of a cranky bride. MOBs have to be prepared to cope with almost *anything*. Fortunately, their years spent mothering have prepared them for almost everything.

As MOB, you will spend an inordinate amount of time shopping for dresses—for yourself and for the bride. The two of you really *will* shop till you drop, and then you'll do it again. Then you'll need the perfect undergarments and the right shoes and pretty handbags . . . and eventually, you'll realize that what the two of you *really* need is a nice, long lunch with some tall, cool drinks.

And that's when you'll reap the rewards of being the MOB. As hectic as planning your daughter's wedding may be, and as tired as you may feel at times, it's an opportunity like no other—to be involved in this important day, and to reconnect with her on such a personal level. It's the stuff moms dream of, and it's all happening for you right now. Take the time to really enjoy it. When the reception winds down and she takes off into her new life, you'll have priceless memories—and the lasting effects—of this time you spent with your girl.

Chapter 1

Your Baby's Engaged!

A mother knows when her daughter's relationship with a certain young man is turning serious. There will be talk of this beau's absolute perfection, a mention or two of his plans for the future, and eventually the M word (that would be *marriage*) starts slipping into conversation. Finally seeing that ring on her finger will be an exciting moment, even if you knew it was coming. You, meanwhile, are automatically appointed mother of the bride. What does this mean to you . . . and to everyone else?

Making the Announcement

Before your daughter and her fiancé break out their bull-horns and start spreading their good news far and wide, who should be told first? (Or more correctly, second—after *you*?) It's important that the people closest to them hear about their impending marriage before the rest of the world does. This might mean that you have to sit on this information until both families have seen the ring with their own eyes.

 **ESSENTIAL**

Express yourself when your daughter announces her big news to you—and be flattered that she came to you right away, even if you're stone-faced about almost everything in life.

First Stop, Mother of the Bride

She comes in your door, all smiles, man in tow, flashing that diamond. See how it sparkles! Look at the size of it! *Ooh* and *aah* and make the biggest fuss you can muster, or else you will later hear how your reaction was not what the happy couple had hoped it would be. For most mothers of the bride, though, hooting and hollering with joy for their daughters won't be a chore. It comes as naturally to them as zeroing in on the perfect dress for the wedding.

Telling the Rest of the Gang

Who's next? Anyone with a vested interest in this wedding should not hear about it through the grapevine. The bride and groom should be the ones to announce the engagement to his folks, obviously. You are not permitted to jump the gun and call your daughter's future in-laws before they even know that they're about to *become* her in-laws. No, no, no. Not your place.

Once the VIPs have been told about the engagement, the world is ready to hear about it. You really can tell anyone and everyone. Make some phone calls to the relatives, or send out a slew of e-mails. You don't need to send out formal announcements, but you surely may if you are moved to do so.

Going Public

If they plan on submitting a picture to the local paper, your daughter and her beau may want to make an appointment with a photographer to have a formal engagement portrait done. Depending on the length of the engagement, they may have some time on their hands before taking care of this, or they could find themselves rushing to a photographer immediately.

What Should It Say?

The announcement will include the bride and groom's information (schooling, occupations, where they're living now, where they will live after the ceremony), along with the names of their parents. Most newspapers simply have forms for the bride and groom to fill out. If the groom's family lives elsewhere, make sure they receive a copy of the engagement photo so that they can put an announcement in their own local newspaper.

⒠ QUESTION

When is the appropriate time to make an announcement in the newspaper?
The engagement announcement (with or without picture) should really appear no sooner than six months prior to the wedding date—three to four months before the big day is closer to an ideal time.

Listing (All) the Parents

If both sets of biological parents happen to be married still, writing the announcement is a piece of cake. You'll simply include where each set of parents lives, and you're done. If one or both sets of parents are divorced, the only effect it has on the announcement is that it will be longer—in order to include all of the parents' names.

For example, if both sets of parents are divorced, and every parent has remarried, the section of the announcement pertaining to them would read: "The bride is the daughter of Mr. and Mrs. Edward Smith of

York, Maine and Mr. and Mrs. Thomas Dolittle of Bakersfield, California. The groom is the son of Mr. and Mrs. Allen Fox of Chicago, Illinois, and Mr. and Mrs. Gregory Brown of Boston, Massachusetts."

If one or more parent has remained single, the announcement would read, "The bride is the daughter of Ms. Valerie Turner of York, Maine, and Mr. and Mrs. Thomas Dolittle of Bakersfield, California. The groom is the son of Mr. and Mrs. Allen Fox of Chicago, Illinois, and Mr. Gregory Brown of Boston, Massachusetts."

Ⓔ **ESSENTIAL**

In the case of naming a divorced, single mother of either the bride or groom, use the name she prefers. She may still prefer to be called Mrs. So-and-So (her former husband's first and last name), or she may simply go by her first and last name, without a "Mrs." or "Ms."

Who *Is* This Young Man?

Because many young women are waiting until they're out of college and established in their careers—sometimes, across the country from where you live—before they settle down with the perfect guy, your daughter may come home already engaged to a man you've never laid eyes on (at least not in person). Of course, you trust her judgment, so you're willing to go on the assumption that he's a great guy. But how can you establish your own relationship with him? After all, the two of you are going to be in each other's lives forever, starting now . . . you want to make sure that you get off to a good start.

Let's Chat, Hon

Sure, he's a responsible adult, and he's proving this by taking on the responsibilities that come along with acquiring a wife and a marriage. You don't have to let it go at that. No, no—you're the mother of the bride, and your subtitle reads, "Supreme Guardian of My Daughter." You have every right to sit down and ask this gentleman some rather probing questions, along the lines of:

- What he does for a living
- His interests and hobbies
- What his plans for the future are (say, if he's in grad school or if he's talking about a move out West)
- Whether he has a former wife and/or children (because they will *hugely* affect your daughter's life)

The first time you meet your daughter's future husband, you want to strike a balance between coming off as a kindhearted soul and having your daughter's best interests at heart. This is sometimes a difficult line to walk, because your daughter's best interests may be served by this man, even if you don't think so. For example, if he's talking about quitting his stable job and entering the Peace Corps (and taking your daughter along with him), your first reaction may be to panic: How are you going to convince her that this is just *wrong*?

Well, that's not really up to you to decide. Sure, most people would like some financial stability in their lives, but you have to try to remember what it was like to be young and in love and to have a real passion for something. Your daughter is probably in complete agreement with her fiancé's ideals, and in fact, his views may be the exact reason she was drawn to him.

Ⓔ ALERT!

Go into your first conversation with this guy with an open mind, and promise yourself not to make any snap judgments. There's lots of time for a full evaluation of him—just not during your initial meeting.

Easy Does It, Mom

So, his job, his kids, his interests, and his plans for the future are fair topics for conversation. What are the things you should *not* plan on asking him about during your first chitchat?

His parents' occupations. It may well come up on its own, but your asking could be seen as an attempt to validate his lineage—especially if your own family is pretty well-off.

His divorce. While you are certainly entitled to know if he's been married before, you are not entitled to every detail of the breakup. Don't ask. You *will* know, eventually.

Exactly **how much he earns.** It's enough to know that he is gainfully employed and/or extremely ambitious. Of course, you don't want to feed and clothe the newlyweds if it turns out he's broke, but keep in mind, minimum wage workers sometimes sock away every penny, and CEOs sometimes run up amazing debt.

His debt. Asking him about his FICO score and/or inquiring about the balances on his major credit cards is out of line. Remember: There's a significant difference between being a mother and being a future mother-in-law. This kind of nosiness at this point in your relationship could keep this guy from ever warming up to you.

And then there are topics that may be very important to you, but are generally divisive, if you don't happen to hold the same beliefs. Don't broach the subjects of politics or religion in your first meeting, if you can help it. Give yourself a chance to like him for who he is first. Chances are, if you're a card-carrying member of the GOP and he answers your question about his personal politics with, "I'm a Democrat, Ma'am," it's going to take you a long, long time to get over it if you've only just met the man. Conversely, if you get to know him before he unveils the liberal side of himself, it might be easier for you to tell yourself that he's *really* a good person, and that counts for something.

Meeting His Folks

The MOB has to be prepared to make friends of the groom's parents for many reasons. For one thing, you may all end up planning this wedding together. For another, you're all going to be related by marriage soon, which means you'll be running into each other at the kids' home for years to come. Lastly, engaged couples want to live their lives in a perfect world—which is difficult to do if they're worried about how their parents will interact.

Let's Be Pals

While some parents can come together and take an automatic liking to one another, it's not always that easy. Especially when parents are from very different financial or social situations, it can be very hard to find a common ground on which to form a friendship. Grooms are sometimes blind to very obvious differences between the folks, while brides tend to get very stressed out about how well everyone will get along.

You can be helpful by initiating conversations where necessary. If, for example, you find yourself eating dinner with the groom's parents (during which you're supposed to be getting to know each other), don't steer all your conversation towards your daughter or your husband. You already know *them*. Branch out. Ask the groom's parents about their hobbies or their work or their other kids. People usually open up (even to strangers) when they're asked about themselves.

You can also lay out a bevy of neutral topics: current events, the weather, the upcoming wedding, even.

Don't sit silently during the entire meal, hoping someone else will get the conversation going. Then again, don't talk incessantly, either.

Ⓔ **ESSENTIAL**

> The truth of the matter is that your daughter shouldn't have to worry about how all of the parents will get along *at all*. No matter what differences you have, you're all adults, capable of making pleasant conversation.

It may be difficult for you to play the role of moderator here, especially if you're on the shy side, but the MOB is typically viewed as a ringleader of sorts. Think of this as one of your responsibilities—to help your daughter bring everyone together.

Argh! These People!

Occasionally, an MOB will find herself tethered to a set of groom's parents whom she just cannot tolerate. Before you launch into a litany of their faults, make sure you're being fair to them.

Things you're right to be irritated by:

- Off-color comments or jokes
- Nasty comments about the kids' engagement
- Boasting (about income, homes, cars, etc.)

You'll notice that there are quite a few things that didn't make the list. Tattoos, bad grammar, and questionable fashion choices are *not* good reasons to completely write off the groom's family—in fact, judging someone on their appearance (or apparent lack of education, in the case of a groom's mother's excessive use of the word "ain't") is downright snobbish. So don't do it.

 FACT

It's true that the world is peppered with some irritating people—but it's just as true that there are some very picky people out there who never give anyone a fair chance. Make sure you're not falling into the latter category.

Now . . . what if you're the one being judged unfairly? You have two choices, and one is better than the other. You can return the snub, or you can kill the snubber(s) with kindness. In returning the rudeness, you're burning a bridge; in being overly kind, you're making yourself look good, and you're also leaving the door open for another try at this whole friendship thing at a later date. You may feel as though you're making yourself look like you're anxious for their approval, but this isn't necessarily the case. What you're really doing is making sure that you're doing your part to get along with your daughter's future in-laws (whom you really won't be spending *that* much time with, anyway). Think of this as a *very* good deed.

Cosponsors

Though the bride's family once headed up most of the wedding and covered the bulk of its expenses, the reality of today's ceremonies and receptions is that the groom's family often pitches in on the cost—which means they also get to have a say-so in the planning.

If you're prepared to pay for the entire wedding, you may want to shut them out of the planning process entirely—but it's not a wise move. Remember, their child is entering into this marriage, too, and if they *want* to take over certain aspects of the wedding, it's best to let them, to avoid wedding-related spats and long-term hard feelings.

ⓔ ESSENTIAL

It may be difficult for you to compromise your idea of the perfect wedding to accommodate the groom's family's ideas. Decide early on which issues are worth a tussle and which aren't. And, of course, keep in mind that in the end, what the bride and groom want should matter the most.

Now, this isn't to say that you should give them the go-ahead to book a bunch of clowns to entertain at an ultraelegant evening reception. What it means is that all of you—the bride and groom included—will need to sit down and discuss what type of wedding this is going to be, the size of the guest list, the menu, the entertainment—*everything*. Advice on how to handle and survive this meeting of the minds is given in Chapter 3.

Whose Wedding Is It?

It's so exciting to think about planning the wedding of your—er, your daughter's dreams, isn't it? Some moms are surprised to find themselves at complete odds with their girls when it comes down to even the most basic planning steps. Are you thinking of a white-tie affair with 300 guests, while your daughter is talking about a wedding in the woods with only immediate family in attendance? You must show her the error of her ways . . . *mustn't* you?

Pull Back, Baby

If the bride is planning on paying for most of this wedding herself, you really can't expect her to change her plans in favor of your wildly different ideas. This is her wedding, after all, especially in the case of the bride and groom who are doing all the legwork and footing the bill . . . they're in charge. Does this mean you can't offer any helpful advice? As long as you can remain helpful (and do not become a buttinski), you can certainly help out when and where the bride requests it of you. Otherwise, zip the lip.

On the other hand, if you (and/or your husband or the bride's dad—whatever the case may be) are paying for most of this wedding, you are entitled to some input. However, you should try as much as possible to respect the bride's general wishes.

It's My Party (Um . . . No, It's Not)

This leads to a discussion on the wedding you wish *you* could have had—if only you and your family could have afforded it then. Now, you're rolling in money (or you have enough, at least, to make your daughter's wedding a lavish event), and darn it, this wedding is going to be everything *you* wanted, whether your daughter agrees or not. (She doesn't realize what she's turning down, and you know she'll be sorry if she misses out on having a huge wedding.) Hijacking her wedding to alleviate your own regrets is a bad idea; you had your turn to be the bride. Let your daughter have her turn now.

Ⓔ **ALERT!**

First things first! You and the bride need to touch base on major wedding issues before anyone signs contracts with vendors. These include the size of the wedding, how formal an affair she's picturing, and her preferred season. The answers to these questions give you a base line to work from.

If she's left the planning completely in your hands, you're *technically* free to do whatever you want. Still, unless she specifically tells you otherwise, it would be in your best interests to double-check certain details with her. (Chicken or beef for dinner? Buffet stations or sit-down meal?) And once you have her opinions, *don't* disregard them, even if you disagree with them. This is a leading cause of daughters and mothers not speaking to one another during the bride's engagement period.

You *Aren't* Made of Money?

You may find yourself talking to a bride who has absolutely no concept of the value of a dollar and/or no idea about how much things cost. She may be the one making out a guest list that seemingly includes a small nation, and you may be the one who has to break the news about the little matter of the *budget* to her. She may retort with, "It's my wedding! We have to do it *my* way!" Mom, you've got your work cut out for you.

If you find yourself in this less-than-enviable position, break it to her gently—but firmly. Perhaps you can still pull off the wedding she wants, if the two of you can agree on how to cut corners in some areas. (She wants 300 people at the reception? Fine. They won't be eating prime rib, for one thing, and they may find themselves standing in a picnic grove instead of the hotel ball-room.) You'll find plenty more tips for careful spending in Chapter 10.

Dealing with the bride who has delusions of grandeur is sometimes tough, but if the two of you can put your heads together and get creative, she may still be able to have a wedding worthy of her dreams—and you'll be able to sleep, knowing that you still have some money left over to pay for . . . you know, *life*.

 **ESSENTIAL**

Yes, you want to give her the wedding of her dreams, but realistically, you can only do so much. It's not wise for you to go into massive debt just so that your daughter can have the most opulent party your hometown has ever seen.

This All Seems Very Familiar . . .

If you've already planned a wedding or two for your other daughters, your first instinct may be to plan the exact same affair for *this* bride-to-be. What's good enough for her sisters is good enough for her. And besides, you can't very well show any favoritism between the girls, so you have to keep their weddings even.

That thought process is admirable; however, "even" doesn't always mean "identical." Chances are, the same members of your family who were at the previous wedding will be at this one, too. You're likely to hear mumbles along the lines of, "Wow, they must really like this place," and, "They must really like the fish here, because we had it at the other reception, too." You're spending an awful lot of money on this—is that really the reaction you want?

Even if your daughter is comfortable with the idea of duplicating her sister's wedding, avoid the urge to do so. Your girls aren't carbon copies of one another, after all; even if they're very much alike, and they've both always wanted very similar weddings, your engaged daughter must have *some* ideas of her own.

Ⓔ **FACT**

> Asking mothers of other recently married brides about their experiences is a great way to get ideas for your daughter's wedding. You can also attend some wedding fairs or shows, pick up some bridal magazines, or see if your chamber of commerce has a catalog of wedding vendors in your area.

Toil or Terrific Times?

Eventually, the novelty of telling everyone that your daughter is engaged will wear off, and you'll realize that you have an *event* to plan. If you've never put a wedding together before, you may be incredibly excited at the prospect of interviewing caterers and photographers, and hopefully, your experience will be trouble-free. Unfortunately, that's not always the case.

Mothers and daughters who are working together sometimes find that the entire planning process is a blast. They get to go shopping together, they start hitting receptions and ceremonies in progress, taking notes on what they like and dislike, and they discuss the plans over nice long lunches. Sounds pretty good.

Of course, for every mother-daughter team enjoying gin and tonics with their Cobb salads after a fun-filled day of shopping for the bride's undergarments, there's a pair who are exhausted and cranky, each of them longing for *alone time*.

Ⓔ ESSENTIAL

It's important to give each other space. If the two of you just can't agree on some aspect of the wedding or you're having trouble finding a vendor to fill your needs, let it go for a day or two—you don't want to mar this time with any unnecessary bickering.

No One Said It Would Be Easy

Don't feel bad if you find yourself not enjoying certain aspects of the planning process. If you're planning a large wedding, especially, you may find yourself feeling like a stranger in a strange land (even though you haven't actually left the confines of your city), shuttling from a caterer's office to the florist to the banquet hall—and trying to make heads or tails of all of the information being thrown at you (and that's *before* you sit down with all of the literature to compare and contrast prices and services).

Keep It Together

If you've never planned anything larger than your annual family holiday party, you may feel a bit overwhelmed once you get into the planning of this wedding. Keep your cool. Some tips for successfully staying on top of this task:

- Get organized. Your level of organization will make or break you.
- Ask questions. Does the banquet manager seem to be speaking in tongues? Make him slow down and address your concerns.
- Take a pal along. Sometimes, having an extra set of eyes and ears is incredibly helpful, especially if every reception site is starting to look exactly the same to you.

In a nutshell, keep all of your information together—in a file, a notebook, a drawer—where it's easily accessible. Don't leave brochures scattered all over your home, or you'll only add to your stress. Don't leave a vendor until you're clear on every issue you wanted to address—these people get paid (at least in part) for answering potential customers' queries. Lastly, *don't* try to do everything yourself. If your daughter isn't available to help out, enlist the help of your sister, a friend, or your husband (if they're willing). Planning a big wedding is a big job, and the more hands to help lighten your load, the better.

Chapter 2

Your Responsibilities

Once you (and others) start referring to yourself as the mother of the bride, you may want to be aware of your official—and unofficial—duties, of which there are many. As hard as planning a wedding can be, just remember it leads up to one big day—and then it's over. Don't lose sight of the other important things in your life while your head is somewhere in the wedding clouds, but try to enjoy this fleeting time while you can.

Traditional MOB Responsibilities

You're one woman who will wear many hats throughout the wedding planning. Bottom line, though, your *real* duty, regardless of the etiquette surrounding the issue, is to get involved as much as the bride wants or needs you to be. Along the same lines, if she *doesn't* want you involved in a certain area of the planning, your duty is to back off.

Typical Official Duties

If the bride and her mom work well together and the bride is looking for some assistance, an MOB usually:

- Establishes a budget for the wedding and the ceremony, if she is making a large contribution toward the final cost
- Helps the engaged couple check out various reception sites and vendors
- Hits the bridal shops with the bride
- Assists in putting the guest list together and works with the groom and/or his family in this regard
- Helps the bridesmaids plan a shower (ideally, by providing a guest list and perhaps a little financial assistance—the girls *should* do everything else)
- Chooses a stunning dress, and lets the groom's mom know all about it so that she won't clash
- Attends parties given in her daughter's honor
- Lends a hand addressing and mailing invitations
- Shuffles guests' names around in an attempt to work out a seating plan for the reception (and then helps fill out the seating cards)

- Helps the bride get dressed for the ceremony
- Participates in the receiving line after the ceremony
- Helps make sure the reception runs smoothly

Many MOBs feel as though they were born to play this take-charge role; others take one look at the workload and hesitate to get involved. If you fall into the latter category, keep in mind that, ideally, you'll only have the chance to get involved in your daughter's wedding *once*, and you may regret passing on some of these opportunities after the vows are said and the rings have been exchanged. This is a once-in-a-lifetime chance to share this incredibly special time with your daughter.

Ⓔ ESSENTIAL

A wedding, of course, is meant to bring people together. If you and your daughter have been leading close but separate adult lives for several years, this is a great opportunity to reconnect with each other.

Unofficial Duties
Your unofficial duties mainly involve the things you do all the time, regardless of who's engaged and who isn't. A wedding tends to take over the lives of anyone who is involved in its planning, though; with so much

talk about dresses and menus, it's easy to let nonbrides and nonwedding events slip through the cracks.

Your *other* responsibilities, then, are to touch base with your engaged daughter every now and then and ask how she's feeling about her impending life change. Let her cry when she gets frustrated with her unsuccessful search for the perfect dress and/or wedding day updo, and take time to talk about *other* important issues (such as how she plans on balancing her relationship with a busy career). Also, try to balance your relationships with other people (such as, say, your other kids, or your husband) with the wedding. Again, these are not necessarily *easy* tasks to accomplish, but they are as important as any of your official duties. Being an MOB means that you have to find more time in your already busy days.

 FACT

Life goes on, even when you're planning a wedding. Make time to chat with the bride's siblings and with your husband, even when you're exhausted from searching for the perfect caterer.

"Oh, this is *not* fair," you may be thinking. "No one can do all of this! Something's gotta give." And you're right. Something will give—you'll be a little less accessible to everyone while you're knee-deep in menus and photographers' price sheets. Just being aware that you'll need to find some way to include life in the wedding season may be enough to keep you on your toes (and to help you avoid cries of neglect from the rest of the family).

What's Expected of You When

Now, that you know what your official duties are, take those duties and carry them into *situations*. Your time to shine as MOB is fast approaching—but this is not a role you can simply jump into on the day of the wedding. No, you'll need plenty of time to ease yourself into an MOB frame of mind, and there's no time like the present. Now's the time to prepare yourself for what lies ahead: the shopping, the guest list, the parties, the wedding, and the reception.

Wedding Preparations

If you're getting involved in the planning, you'll be a valuable asset to the bride and groom, evaluating reception halls, interviewing vendors, and keeping in contact with various wedding businesses. You may be called upon to work out details and sign contracts. Your best bet here is to educate yourself so that you can be an informed consumer; your next best bet is to only work with vendors who are willing to meet your needs. Settling for a banquet hall that doesn't offer the services you're looking for just because you and the bride love its entryway is going to set you off sooner or later.

In addition', you'll need to put a guest list together for your side of the family, and be in contact with the groom's family regarding their guest list. You'll give them a number to work with, and tell them when you'll need the names. Make sure you have the correct number to avoid any potentially sticky spots. For example, if the groom's mother submits her list to you (and it's within her limit), you shouldn't call her and ask her to eliminate some of the guests because your math was off. It could well be that she's already told these people that they are invited.

(E) ESSENTIAL

The bride may ask you to help out with shopping trips—including her registry. If she's never lived on her own, she may have no idea what she needs (the nonstick set of pots and pans)—and what she *doesn't* need (the silver candelabra).

Pre-Wedding Parties

The bride's attendants are traditionally expected to host a shower for her. If the wedding is only months away and there's been no mention of a party, go ahead and give them a little nudge—or plan it yourself. (Though etiquette states that the bride's mom should not host her shower, it's more common these days for people to toss etiquette and do what's easiest and most convenient.) If the bridesmaids do have everything under control, you may be asked to provide them with a guest list.

Should the bride's friends invite you to her bachelorette party, you may want to think twice about attending—depending on how you feel about wild behavior. Most bachelorettes plan on a lot of drinking, references to the male anatomy, and/or a male stripper or two. If this sounds like your idea of a good time, count yourself in. If not, skip it.

 FACT

> It's the prerogative of the bride's family to host the first engagement party—but you're not *required* to do so. If you do choose to honor the happy couple, think about planning it for six to eight months prior to the wedding, and include the groom's family in the guest list.

Wedding Eve

Often, the wedding rehearsal is held the night before the wedding (otherwise, it's held several nights prior to the big event). Every member of the wedding party (this includes *you*) should be there, because this is akin to a dress rehearsal—no one wants to see bridesmaids wandering around during the ceremony because they have no idea where they should be standing or what they should be doing. Ditto for the parents of the bride and groom. Sure, you know how to walk down an aisle, but do you know what you're supposed to do once the ceremony begins? (No, you're not supposed to straighten her veil and poof her train—unless you're doubling as the matron of honor.) Make sure you're at the rehearsal.

The rehearsal dinner follows the run-through of the ceremony. The groom's family normally takes care of the details surrounding this event, so all you have to do is show up and be charming.

Wedding Day

When the big day finally arrives, you'll be the bride's right-hand woman. She'll need you to help her prepare herself for the ceremony, which may include driving her to the hairdresser's, helping her with her makeup, and assisting her with the big dress. You'll also be dealing with various hired help (the florist will pop in with a huge delivery and the photographer will be shuffling your entire family around) and bridesmaids to boot.

At the ceremony, you will most likely be seated in the first row before the bride enters the building. Whatever the case, once things get going, all you have to do is sit and watch. Take the time to look around at the results of all your planning and then sit back and enjoy the ceremony—it will be over before you know it. When the ceremony ends, you'll exit directly behind the wedding party. At the reception, your job is to be a charming hostess and make sure that everything goes according to plan—*or,* if something's amiss, to take it up with the banquet manager.

Ⓔ ALERT!

> This can be a very stressful time for MOBs. Don't take it out on the bride. She's stressed, too, and getting on her case is only going to cause major friction between the two of you. Try not to be too controlling here. Try to work at *her* pace.

How to Avoid the Pushy MOB Label

Despite your best intentions, you may hear your daughter complaining about how bossy you've become since her engagement. Your first reaction may be to tack it up to the bridal stress that sometimes strikes young women on their way to the altar. While this explanation may account for part of the problem . . . take a good, honest look at your own behavior (just for kicks). There's a chance—and it's just a *chance*, mind you—that you're veering into controlling MOB territory. Some moms really do end up carrying the entire burden of the planning all by themselves, and do a great job of it—but some moms make things extraordinarily difficult for everyone around them, including the bride. To find out if this is you, ask yourself the following questions:

• Have you been picking out reception halls, planning menus, and choosing dresses without even consulting the bride on her preferences?

• Is the groom completely in the dark about his own wedding, even though he keeps asking questions and continuously offers his help?

• Have you seen your husband lately, or is he avoiding you until after the wedding?

• Do you feel like you're the only person who seems to be losing sleep, wondering if this wedding will turn out perfectly?

• Are you convinced that planning this wedding is going to assure you a place in heaven (because no one else is working as hard on planning this event as you think they should be)?

Ⓔ ESSENTIAL

Be good to yourself, and be good to those around you. This wedding will be smashing no matter what—but you'll have a better time at the reception if your family is still speaking to you.

How can you avoid this syndrome? From the get-go, you need to decide how much of the planning you're going to take on and which duties will be handled by the bride and groom. Make a schedule for yourself so that you aren't trying to book twelve vendors in one week, and take some time out from the planning when it gets to be too much. If you start early enough, you'll be able to pace your planning so that it doesn't all pile up on you three months prior to the wedding date—when finding vendors with open dates will be difficult and trying to plan pre-wedding parties *and* a wedding simultaneously will be incredibly stressful.

Keeping Dad in the Loop

Remember earlier in this chapter, when other family members and their needs were discussed? Keeping the family connected while you're busy planning a wedding can be a tough task, especially if you happen to be married to a man who'd rather hide in his den than discuss wedding details. But remember, he might have some ideas of his own to contribute, and since he's most likely going to play a big part in constructing the budget, it's best to make sure you two are on the same page.

The Budget

If you and your husband are paying for most of this wedding, you need to sit down and discuss how much you're going to end up shelling out. No matter which one of you normally handles the family finances, it's important to be in agreement about how much you will be spending on this event. If one of you is normally a big spender (i.e., he likes to buy himself all the latest tools and gadgets, or you can't pass up a new pair of shoes), you need to realize that you'll probably have to cut back on the shopping—at least for now. Otherwise, you could find yourself flat broke after paying for those purchases *and* your daughter's wedding.

Does He *Want* In?

If you're sitting at the dinner table and your husband is just full of ideas for this wedding (he knows a great restaurant or a fabulous photographer), let him join the planning. Even if some of his ideas are notoriously suspect (his last suggestion for a night out included taking a mime class), give him a chance to wow you with his brilliance. While many dads choose to leave all of the planning to the bride's mom, some men really do want to help out. Don't deny him the chance.

 FACT

> Another way to get Dad involved is to give him some specific tasks to work on. Let him set up appointments with vendors. Ask him to compile a guest list of his own family members. The most important thing is to let him participate if he wants to.

Including Your Ex

Maybe you and your former husband are best friends and you can't foresee a single problem with the two of you contributing your time and money to this wedding.

Or maybe you can't stand the mention of his name. As far as you're concerned, there's no reason to include him in the planning, and it would be detrimental to *everyone* to have the two of you working together on this.

Since MOBs usually take the reins of planning the wedding, you certainly are not obligated to put yourself in a position that's only going to make your job harder. However, you are going to have to find a way to communicate with him on certain issues—such as his side of the guest list, and whether he's contributing to this wedding. He should also be filled in on the dates and times of the rehearsal and the wedding as soon as possible.

Ⓔ ALERT!

If you really, truly feel it's in everyone's best interests to have someone act as liaison between you and your ex, do it. It would be far worse for the two of you to revisit old arguments and have the bride be forced to deal with *that* during her engagement.

If your divorce was *really* bad, you may feel as though even speaking to this man on the phone is impossible for you to do without developing a weeklong migraine. It's all right to ask your daughter to intervene (as long as you don't preface the request with, "Honey, you know how much I hate your dad . . . "). Be aware that she may accuse you of being juvenile, but don't even enter into that argument. Ignore her accusation and hand over the task of communications with her dad to her.

Above and Beyond

While there are, of course, quite a few tasks that are traditionally *expected* of the mother of the bride, there are plenty of chores that you won't find listed in any etiquette book. As the wedding approaches, you'll have your hands full dealing with situations that are common to every MOB. How you'll handle them will be *un*commonly courageous—and will earn you the title of MOB Extraordinaire.

Oh, Those Bridesmaids!

Unfortunately, some brides find that their bridesmaids cause them so much trouble and so much heartache that eloping starts sounding like a good option. Whether your daughter has chosen family or friends (or a mix of the two camps) to fill the chiffon dresses, there always seems to be at least one who chooses to be disagreeable about everything—about the getup, about the bridal shower, or even about the date and time of the wedding (seems it's inconvenient to her schedule and she'll show up when she can).

What can an MOB do to help in this situation? First, you need to let your daughter try to handle it herself. It's really best if she can appeal to this unreasonable maid woman-to-woman, and settle things that way. If the attendant in question is persistent in her quest to drive the bride insane, go ahead and step in—as long as the offenses are serious enough. (A bridesmaid who has expressed her disdain for the color of the dresses on one occasion is easier for the bride to ignore than a maid of honor who is talking incessantly about taking a vacation the week before the wedding and flying back into town an hour before the ceremony.)

Ⓔ ESSENTIAL

Be extra careful when dealing with a member of the groom's family. If the bride can't appeal to her reasonable side, perhaps her own mother can. If that fails, you're free to approach her, but remember your daughter has to deal with her for the rest of eternity.

There are few people in this world more intimidating than an MOB who's *had it*. It's an *honor* for a woman to be included in a wedding party—reminding the offender of this fact, and of the fact that it's not her *right* to be included (which implies that she can easily be *ex*cluded), may be enough to stop her behavior.

Oh, Those In-Laws!

Another bunch who may irk your daughter before the wedding: the in-laws. While it's understandable that tensions are high before the wedding (and to be fair, you have to acknowledge that whether these people are truly involved in the planning or not, their child is getting married, too), sometimes the in-laws' behavior goes beyond the realm of what reasonable brides can tolerate.

A groom's mother, for example, may bitterly contest everything about the wedding—the church where the ceremony will be held, the bridesmaids' colors, the season, the reception site . . . you name it. The MOG who isn't paying for a blessed thing is much easier to deal with than one who is going halvsies on the shindig. Sure, she's irritating, but since you and the bride don't have to work out any details with her (other than the guest list), your exposure to her will be minimal. Let her go her own way, and you and your daughter can go yours. Trying to force a sourpuss into a happy wedding mood is only going to backfire.

ⓔ ALERT!

If wedding-related financial issues between the bride and the groom's parents can't be resolved, the bride may have to think about returning any money they've contributed and planning a smaller wedding. Assure her this *will* be worth it in the long run.

If your daughter finds herself dealing with in-laws who are paying for at least part of the wedding and they simply disregard all of the bride's wishes, is it right for you to step in? It depends on how bold you're feeling, and it depends on the groom's parents, too. If you suspect that there's no malicious intent on their part and that your daughter could very easily straighten things out by speaking to them, then stay back. On the other hand, if you know your daughter has already had a tete-a-tete or two with her future mother-in-law, sometimes a meeting of the moms is in order. The groom's mother may be able to intimidate a young bride, but she doesn't scare you. Lay it on the line with this woman: This wedding is neither yours nor the MOG's, and the bride's wishes should be respected.

Oh, That Bride!

While this is supposed to be a wonderful time in your daughter's life, and she's supposed to be the grande dame of the ball for a number of months, some MOBs notice a slight personality change. Or, truth be told, the personality change is huge—and it's horrific. Out-of-control brides wreak havoc on everyone in sight—their attendants, their siblings, their coworkers, their grooms, and even (gasp!) their moms. Are you supposed to ignore this? After all, the wedding will be over (someday) and she'll return to her normal self, so what's wrong with letting her run amok for now? Every bride does it.

Hmm . . . not true. And even if it *were* true, it's not right. Or good. Or healthy.

You're a mom. You've been looking out for this girl from day one. Don't stop now, just because she's so pretty in white taffeta. What to do about it? She's an adult, after all, and you can't exactly ground her from her wedding. But you *can* tell her that an engagement ring does not confer upon her the right to treat others with disdain. You *can* tell her that her lousy treatment of you is unacceptable. Why would you be so mean? (Be prepared to answer this question, because she'll throw it at you.) It's not being mean, really, it's being *honest*. She won't thank you for this advice (not until *she* has to deal with a bratty bride), but everyone else in her life will admire how levelheaded and rational you are—and they'll also applaud your fearlessness at confronting the pugilistic bride.

Ⓔ FACT

Bride or no, bratty behavior is unacceptable. Some of her friends and family members will shrug this conduct off and tack it up to pre-wedding mania; others, though, *won't*. You're just trying to make her realize that being a bride is not akin to being a dictator.

Calling for Backup

Chapter 1 briefly mentioned one of the best tricks in an MOBs bag: assistance (in one form or another). Even the best and most enthusiastic party planners rely on help (which is *why* they're the best and most enthusiastic), because one woman simply cannot do everything. You may find that your out-of-town daughter drops this wedding in your lap with one instruction: "Plan it." Or your daughter may not have any interest whatsoever in planning her wedding, but she knows that if you take care of the details, it will be beautiful. However this wedding has ended up on your to-do list, you'll need all the help you can get—with a few caveats.

Recruiting Helpers

If you have a sister or a good friend who might be willing to help out, ask her. Planning the wedding is something that people generally get excited over— and most will be flattered that you would trust them to be of assistance. Give them the numbers of some vendors; ask if they can set up appointments; bring them along to check out the various sites and wares. You'll be bombarded with wedding information and having a helper with you can be helpful for a few reasons:

- She may ask questions you hadn't thought of
- She may see something you missed (like water damage or a chef with dirty hands—ew!)
- She may present a point of view you hadn't considered (for example, she may be vegetarian and find herself looking at a menu without a single nonmeat option)

Her thoughts and opinions might well save you from making some big errors.

Professional Help

Can't find anyone who's any help to you? Your sister is 300 miles away, and your friends are too busy. You asked your husband and he just laughed. Are you doomed to wander from caterer to caterer, doomed to an existence of solitary taste tests?

Ⓔ QUESTION

How can I find a good wedding planner?
Ask around. If you have friends who have recently enlisted the help of a consultant, they can tell you about their experiences. You can also hit the bridal show circuit. Check the Better Business Bureau's Web site to make sure a planner is reputable.

Give some thought to hiring a wedding planner. These professionals know the territory, and can usually lead you in the right direction. They'll take your budget into account, try to get a feel for what you're thinking, and get to work. Any planner who's been in the business for a while knows the local vendors, and can advise you as to which ones are reputable and well worth your money. Your planner might even have a good enough relationship with some of them that he or she can cut you a pretty sweet deal for some services.

Once you have a planner in mind, schedule an initial interview to discuss the budget and to get an idea of what he or she is like. Then decide whether you'd want to work with this person. Remember that wedding planners provide a whole range of services. You may be looking for someone to simply advise you in certain matters of etiquette, or you may be looking for someone to plan the entire event; you need to know if this particular planner offers the services you're after. You'll also need to have an estimate of your total wedding budget and make sure the planner is willing to work within it. Here are some good questions to get you started:

- How long have you been in business?
- How much (or how little) of the wedding will you plan?
- How many weddings do you plan per month?
- Do you have a staff?
- What's your fee? (Is it a flat fee or percentage of the total cost of the wedding?)
- Do you have any references from recent clients?

Keep in mind that if a wedding planner takes on too many weddings, *someone's* big day is likely to fall through the cracks. Logically speaking, it would be nearly impossible to take on more than two weddings per weekend—so planners who boast that they plan twelve weddings every month may not necessarily be the best choice—unless they have a support staff filling in for them.

Don't be afraid to ask a lot of questions and to really get a conversation going with this woman (or man). If you're hiring a wedding planner to put an entire wedding together, you need to know that the two of you can work well together, and that you'll be able to communicate your ideas effectively. If you get the feeling that the two of you will be butting heads for the next several months (and on your dime, no less) walk away.

Chapter 3
Money Matters

Might as well jump into the topic of money. Or, more specifically, *whose* money is supposed to pay for *what*. You may have already perused some bridal etiquette books, and you may have broken into a cold sweat when you read, "The bride who comes from a proper family will indeed expect her parents to pay for the entire ceremony and reception. And it will be *grand!*" Don't panic. There's a new reality out there for parents who can't fathom dropping their life's savings on a wedding.

Bride's Family: Traditional Expenses

For those of you who cling to tradition, you'll want and need to know what it is you're hanging onto, at least as far as this wedding is concerned. Once your daughter comes home and announces her engagement, you can open your purse (or your vault). You may want to host an engagement party . . . or you may not want to, once the wedding draws closer and you realize what you'll be paying for (almost *everything*). The wedding spending spree starts right here, right now.

Toasting the Happy Couple

The bride's family traditionally hosts the first engagement party, but this is not an obligation. If you choose not to host this soiree, make it very clear to those who are inquiring about such a fete. If, for example, the groom's mother asks whether you're planning a party to honor the happy couple, and you know you aren't, don't beat around the bush and say, "Well, we haven't really decided," or worse, "Yes, I think we'll probably get around to it." The MOG might be asking you because *she* would like to host the party—but classy lady that she is, she doesn't want to step on any toes.

What does the engagement party entail, financially? That depends on whether you're planning a formal or informal affair. You can reasonably have a backyard barbecue engagement party, or you can book the swankiest club in town and host a black-tie shindig. An at-home party is obviously cheaper in every respect: the food, the entertainment, the free use of your own home.

The cost of this party will also depend on how many guests you're inviting, which is entirely up to you. You'll want to include members of the groom's family, of course, but beyond that, you can invite the entire town—or no one else. Everyone you invite to the engagement party, though, must also be invited to the wedding. (More on this in Chapter 4.)

Ⓔ ESSENTIAL

You do not need to send formal, profession-ally printed invitations for an engagement party unless it's a formal event. Save that money for another wedding-related expense (there will be many). Store-bought invites will suffice for this occasion.

Now for the Real Bill . . .

Relatively speaking, the cost of the engagement party is *nothing* compared to the cost of the wedding. What else does the bride's family pay for—tra-ditionally? The bride herself usually pays for wedding gifts for the groom and her attendants and for the groom's wedding ring. Her parents are traditionally responsible for:

- The bride's dress (and, of course, the MOB's dress)
- Most of the flowers
- Musicians for the church and the reception
- Fee for the church
- Transportation for the wedding party
- Photographer and videographer
- Invitations
- Reception hall
- Food
- Drinks

Ⓔ FACT

Weddings can be incredibly expensive, and for many, many families of many, many brides, it's just not feasible or realistic to fork over somewhere in the neighborhood of $25,000 for *one day's* amusement. (*Especially* if the bride has sisters who'll be walking down the aisle anytime soon.)

You're suppressing your laughter, because this is obviously some sort of joke. You'll just flip to the end of this chapter to find the real list of your expenses. Don't bother. The bride's family really *does* cover all of these expenses in a traditional arrangement. Now, the amount of money the bride's family ends up shelling out is dependent on several factors: the type of wedding (ultraformal? semiformal? informal?), the size of the guest list, and how creative the bride and her mom are when it comes to cutting costs. These factors will vary from wedding to wedding and might not end up being as daunting as you originally thought they would be.

The Groom's Family

There they are, counting their riches and snickering over their good fortune at being parents of the groom (at least at *this* particular wedding). But hang on—these people have a few financial obligations of their own. The groom himself is usually responsible for wedding gifts and ring for the bride, gifts for the groomsmen, and the honeymoon. His parents take care of the following expenses:

- Officiant's fee
- Flowers: bride's bouquet, mothers' and grandmothers' corsages, boutonnieres for groomsmen
- Rehearsal dinner

"That's *it*?" you ask. "Where's the rest?" Well, in a traditional setup, *you've* already paid for the rest. Is this fair? Perhaps in the days of dowries and arranged marriages—and heck, in the days where weddings were thrown together in someone's home—it was a suitable arrangement. However, in contemporary times, the uneven balance of the bride's family paying for the bulk of the wedding seems outdated. Tradition is sometimes overrated, wouldn't you say?

Today's Reality

If your daughter is earning more money than you ever dreamed she would, should you still be expected to pay for her wedding? And what about the groom's parents? Wouldn't it be ideal if the two families could come together and agree to divvy up the final bill? It would certainly lighten your financial load, and it would also allow the groom's family to get involved in the planning of the wedding. Fortunately (for you), the *realities* of who pays for what in a typical wedding are not always bound by tradition.

Common Sense

Today, more couples are waiting until they're a bit older and established in their careers before they get married. Where once a bride was either fresh out of college or even younger when she took her wedding vows, it's more likely these days to see a bride who has been out in the real world, earning some real bucks for quite some time. As a result, she can afford to contribute extensively to her own wedding—or perhaps (along with her fiancé) even pay for the entire thing. Your parents may have scrimped and saved for your wedding—but it doesn't have to be that way for today's brides, and a daughter who is managing her own money probably would feel terrible about accepting *too* much from her parents. After all, unlike brides of yesteryear, this girl knows firsthand the value of a buck.

Another bonus for a bride who has the money to spend on her own wedding is that she can either go all out and plan an extravagant affair, or she might go to the other extreme (because, remember, she knows all about money) and plan a very simple affair. Whatever the case, if the bride and groom are bound and determined to pay for most of this wedding by themselves, don't wallow in guilt. If you want to offer them a contribution, they may accept it with glee (after all, money is money), or they may refuse it. Don't push the issue. You don't want to end up fighting over expenses, especially when you don't need to.

 ALERT!

> You shouldn't feel guilty about your daughter paying for her own wedding. It's not a matter of what you're *not* doing for her—it's what she's able to do for *herself*, which is exactly the way women of her generation have been raised to think.

One Big Happy Planning Session

All right, so what about the bride and groom who are able to pay for *part* of the wedding, but who are also expecting some help from one or both sets of parents? How do you go about splitting the bill three ways? Does it have to be *exactly* even? Who takes the initiative on which parts? First off, you need to know if the groom's parents are even interested in making a major contribution to the wedding. *You* will not call and ask the groom's parents; it's up to your daughter and her beau to take care of these arrangements. Then, several situations present themselves:

- You and the groom's family can simply hand your wedding contributions to the bride and groom, and the kids can go ahead and plan their wedding.
- The groom's family might agree to pay for certain aspects of the wedding (for example, they might want to pay for the bar bill and the limousine—or any other expense of their choice).
- You might go ahead and plan the entire wedding and then accept payment from the bride and groom and/or the groom's family.

What happens in the end will be the result of who trusts whom and who feels comfortable doing what. In other words, if you and the groom's family barely know one another, don't expect them to hand you a check for several thousand dollars a whole year before the reception.

Did Someone Say *Happy?*

Alas, what happens when three different parties converge in an attempt to pull off the wedding of *everyone's* dreams? Sometimes, the end result is a fairy-tale wedding; other times, the planning process is so nightmarish that the bride and groom wish they had eloped. Your role as MOB, you'll remember, is to help your daughter. You're trying to help her pull off the wedding *she* wants. The groom's family, however, may not be in touch with this minimum standard of conduct, and if they're pitching in on the event, they may just feel as though they've been given the green light to do whatever they want. And worse, their intentions might be pure—yes, the MOG just might think she's *helping* by hiring a caller for a square dance at the formal reception your daughter is planning.

Ⓔ ESSENTIAL

Try not to judge the groom's family—or their intentions—too harshly. Everyone has different tastes. As long as they mean well, find a way to work it out without establishing a lifetime of hard feelings between the two families.

While it's very difficult to set ground rules for adults who are laying their own money down on the table in an effort to assist in the planning and lessen the financial strain on your pocketbook, it is possible to be tactful about the whole situation. Read on . . .

Be Nice, Now

So, how does one diplomatically dictate the terms of planning? *Very carefully.* MOBs—even when they're the nicest women on the block—are sometimes viewed suspiciously by others, as though they're up to something. The groom's family may feel as though you're trying to act as puppet master if you approach them on *any* issue in a less–than appropriate manner.

Your job here is to stay out of the head planner's seat, even if you really are the one who is doing all the legwork and making all the calls for your daughter. The bride and groom are the ones who need to express their wants and needs to his parents. After all, the money the groom's parents are handing over is really a gift to the happy couple—it doesn't belong to you, per se, even if its real purpose is to alleviate *your* financial burden.

You really shouldn't get involved in this particular matter until the bride gives you the go-ahead. (Hopefully, she will have made the first foray into the topic with her future in-laws already.) Once the bride and groom have some idea of where his family stands on the issue of money as it relates to this wedding, they can either give you the go-ahead to contact the future in-laws, or they'll let you know that you're on your own.

(E) ALERT!

Once you're labeled as a pushy MOB—even if you don't truly deserve the title—there's no going back. Relations between you and the groom's family will be strained until after the wedding, and perhaps well beyond that point.

Finding the Money

Where are you going to get the money to pay for your part of this wedding, anyway? Years ago, it was common to hear about families saving for their daughters' weddings—nowadays, a bridal fund is more likely to be something a daughter only *hopes* exists. If you're short an entire fund for the wedding, but you're planning on writing at least a check or two to cover some of the costs, you might have some ideas swirling around in your mind. Are they good ones or bad ones?

Keep the House

Selling your house to pay for your daughter's wedding is a fairly extreme idea. A house is likely to be one of your biggest assets, so trading it in, in order to treat 500 guests to filet mignon is a bad idea. Refinancing is probably not the best idea, either, unless you were planning on doing so before your daughter's engagement. Here's why: When you refinance your home, you get a check (and a lower mortgage rate—at least temporarily), which is great if you have big bills to pay (bills related to a wedding, for example)—but you're trading the equity you already have. In most cases, you're essentially starting from square one, as though you just bought the house. This is just fine if you're not planning on selling anytime soon (you can kiss your profit goodbye if you try to sell right away), and if you don't fall into the habit of cashing in on your home's value every time you spend a little too much money here or there.

Home Equity Loans

Home equity loans can be lifesavers . . . or they can come back to haunt you. In this transaction, homeowners can borrow a percentage of the value of their home to pay off higher-interest loans or large debts. The interest on the loan is usually tax deductible. Again, this may be a good way to go if you're careful with your money to begin with . . . which maybe you aren't if you have to borrow against your home to pay off your wedding debt. (Not a judgment call, mind you— just a thought.)

Ⓔ FACT

Folks who refinance to pay off bills trade their equity in their home for a quick payoff elsewhere . . . which can lead to spending trouble if you're quick to say, "Well, I'm out of debt. Guess I can afford to spend some more!"

The advantage is that you're paying less interest on your wedding debt right now. The downside is that you're paying off this loan for thirty years. Also, if the loan exceeds 100 percent of the value of your home, the interest is *not* tax deductible, which means you've entered into a standard loan. If you fall behind on your payments for whatever reason, you might find yourself packing your bags.

Cash? Credit?

So, is it advisable, then, to pay cash for a wedding? Believe it or not, it isn't—at least not *literally*. While it is smart to set a budget and a spending limit while simultaneously deciding which areas of the wedding are priority issues (does your daughter want stretch limos for the wedding party and the families, or would she rather spend that money on an open bar?), it's not wise to hand over cold hard cash to pay the bills.

Ⓔ ESSENTIAL

Using your credit card carefully could help you out if there's a dispute with a vendor. However, it's incredibly *unwise* to use credit to go on a wedding-spending bender by purchasing items you'd never buy otherwise (like a $15,000 designer original wedding dress). Set your budget early on *and stick to it.*

Whenever possible, try to pay deposits by credit card—*but keep track of what you're spending*. Once you give cash or a check to a vendor, your money is out of your hands—and if there's a problem in the future (say, the caterer decides he'd rather use your money to take a vacation instead of feeding your daughter's wedding guests), it's very possible that you'll never see a refund. Conversely, if you've used your plastic, your credit card company will help you fight any bogus charges. The chances of your being reunited with your dough are much better in this instance. And of course, *always, always* get a receipt and put it away safely (not in the bottom of your pocketbook).

Pay at the Door, Please

All right, with all this talk about who's paying for what and how expensive things are, you might be thinking that this book has missed an obvious fact: Most brides receive *a lot* of money as wedding gifts, so obviously, the bride and groom can just pay off their ceremony and reception bills that way. Ooh . . . not such a hot idea.

A Gift Is a Gift

Some engaged couples (and their moms, too, unfortunately) have been known to sit down and figure out to the penny how much it will cost to feed and water and entertain each guest (estimating each guest's intake of stuffed mushrooms and martinis). When the newlyweds sit down to open their gifts, they expect that their guests will have done the *same* accounting homework and will have included enough cash in an envelope to cover the cost of their night out on the town. This is just common courtesy, isn't it?

Wrong-o, Mom. Don't encourage your daughter to spend more of her money on her wedding because she'll make it all back in wedding gifts. For one thing, it encourages irresponsible spending habits, and for another, it's just wrong. Guests are *guests*. If your cousin shows up giftless, that's all right in the world of etiquette; you ostensibly invited her because you want her to share in the day—not because she's loaded.

 **ALERT!**

> Your guests are obligated to show up if they have RSVP'd in the affirmative. That's *all*. They are in no way obligated to pay what amounts to a cover charge to attend your daughter's wedding.

Your daughter should expect nothing, and then she'll be pleasantly surprised with her bounty—instead of having unrealistically high expectations and being wildly disappointed.

Travel and Lodging

If your aunt is traveling from Australia to attend the wedding, are you supposed to pay for her airfare and her hotel? No, you're not. When a guest receives an invitation to a distant wedding, it's up to her to decide whether she can reasonably afford to make the trip. If she can't (or simply doesn't want to spend that kind of money), she'll stay home that weekend. If she does end up coming, she shouldn't complain about how much money she's spent on this wedding. Of course, you can't control her mouth, so if she's a disagreeable sort who's traveled all that way simply to irritate you, welcome her pleasantly, then stay away from her.

Destination Wedding Expenses

How do the costs for a destination wedding differ from a typical hometown event? In truth, you may get off a little easier—if the bride and groom can cover the cost of this wedding themselves. In order to make your decision on whether you're going to throw your hat (your banker's hat *or* your planner's hat) into this ring, you'll want some specifics.

The Lowdown on Destinations

A destination wedding is a wedding that takes place in a far-off location, whether that is a resort that specializes in such occasions, or an out-of-the-way vacation spot that holds a special meaning for the couple. Weddings of this nature are becoming more popular with the current generation of brides for several reasons:

- They're different from typical weddings back home.
- They're often held in a location known for its beauty.
- Couples can make this an intimate affair without offending the extended family.

If your daughter has dreams of getting married on the beach, or in the Alps, or on a dude ranch, she might be cooking up something creative for her wedding day. Though many brides opt to head for resorts that routinely host destination weddings, other brides want their wedding day to be as different as possible from anything else anyone has ever seen. Until you hear the final word from the bride on this matter, all bets are off. (Don't start packing your sarong and sunscreen just *yet*.) At the same time, don't assume that because she's talking about a destination wedding that it's going to be a huge expense—she might be talking about driving to a little inn two or three hours down the road.

Ⓔ FACT

Traveling to far-flung places requires *a lot* of thought. Does the bride really want to spend an entire day in the air to reach the altar? Does her foreign location have a residency requirement for marriage? Encourage her to do some very thorough research on her destination of choice.

Your Obligation

Wherever this wedding takes place, you already know that the bride's family typically covers the bulk of the wedding expenses. Guess what? When a bride and groom choose a destination wedding, *they're* usually held responsible for the cost of their own wedding. Why? Because getting married on a beautiful beach or in a mountaintop lodge or on a ranch is *their* choice. And as a result of the research they did to find this dream location, they'll know whether they can afford this venture—or not.

The planning for this event may be more difficult (if they're headed where no bride or groom has gone before), or it may be incredibly easy (some resorts offer wedding packages complete with planners to take care of every detail). Your daughter and her fiancé should know what they're getting into before booking reservations.

Ⓔ ESSENTIAL

In addition to the location, the bride and groom will have to decide if they're shooting for a formal wedding or an informal one, and whether they want to invite only immediate family members or everyone they know.

Guest Responsibilities

Since destination weddings are the new kids on the wedding planning block, suffice it to say that there is still some debate over who should ultimately pay which of the guests' bills. It's safe to say that everyone should plan on paying for their own *travel* expenses. Other expense decisions (such as lodging and food) should be made on a case-by-case basis. If the bride and groom can afford to swing this tab, they should give some thought to doing so. On the other hand, many destination brides argue that their out-of-town guests would be paying for their own hotel rooms if they were traveling to a traditional wedding in the bride's hometown, so there's no reason not to expect this of them.

There's logic to both sides of the discussion—the important thing is that no matter what the bride and groom decide, their guests should know well in advance of making *their* decision to attend the wedding.

You Can Join Us Now

If your daughter has chosen a destination wedding, you might be fretting over the fact that your family and friends may not be able to make the trip. The perfect solution? A post-wedding reception! Hang on, Mom. It may not be as perfect as you're thinking.

If the bride and groom chose to take their vows in a remote location because they wanted their wedding to be as intimate as possible, what kind of message does that send to the guests you're inviting to the after-the-fact reception? If they weren't privileged enough to witness the vows, why should they come running *now* to celebrate the union?

On the other hand, if the bride and groom had an extensive guest list for their destination wedding and only a handful of guests were *able* to attend, a reception at home makes sense. Guests may have already sent gifts, or they might bring them to this party. (Or they might not. Remember, guests are never obligated to give presents.)

Post-Wedding Reception Invitations

If you're hosting a post-wedding reception, you can go as swanky or as down-home as you'd like, though most of these parties tend to be cocktails-and-cake events. For a formal reception, you should send out formal, printed invitations at least a month before the party. The wording on an invitation to this party reads:

Mr. and Mrs. Timothy Tuttle
request the pleasure of your company
at a reception
in honor of
Mr. and Mrs. Harold Hart
on Sunday, August tenth
Two thousand and six
at two o'clock in the afternoon
Sarasota Yacht Club
Sarasota, Florida

If the groom's family is pitching in on this event, add their names below yours:

Mr. and Mrs. Timothy Tuttle
And
Mr. and Mrs. Mitchell Murray . . .

Chapter 4
The Parties!

Most brides find themselves in the guest of honor seat at a party or two (or three or four) in the months leading up to the big event. What are *your* duties as far as these soirees are concerned? It depends on how involved you want to be, how involved the hostess of the party wants you to be, and on the party itself. This chapter will give you the skinny on some of the pre-wedding parties you might be involved with—one way or another.

Party Planning Basics

Once your daughter becomes engaged, there will be parties galore. While in some cases the only thing you will be responsible for is showing up with your best MOB smile, in other cases you will be involved with much of the planning. In fact, the pre-wedding parties are where you might cut your party planning teeth and gain valuable research skills that you can carry over into planning the wedding itself. This all depends, of course, on how large and/or how formal each event will be. If you're thinking about hosting an at-home engagement party, for example, you'll have to either find a caterer or come up with a mathematical equation to figure out how many gallons of macaroni salad and how many packages of rolls you'll need for fifty hungry guests. These particular planning skills may or may not come in handy for planning the reception.

Ⓔ ALERT!

Don't go way over your budget when planning a party. It's very easy to start overspending once you're presented with the most magnificent options. Stick to your plan, and don't allow yourself to be pulled into anything that you might regret later. (Remember, you're going to be shelling out for a *wedding* soon.)

File It Under *Organized*

An organizational system, whether that means colored folders, computer files, and/or an actual file cabinet, will be your best friend when you're putting an event like this together. Organization is the key to successful party planning. You'll never attend a creative, brilliantly planned party and hear the hostess say, "You know, it just all took care of itself. I don't even remember the name of the caterer." (If she *does* say this, she's not telling the truth.)

If you've been suffering from some sort of affliction that necessitates *dis*organization on a daily basis, and worse, this has been a lifelong problem, you're probably thinking that there's no hope for you. Disorder *is* order for you, and you can't change now. Wrong, Mom. There's always hope for even the most diehard clutter lovers. How does one get organized quickly and painlessly?

Start small. Don't try to compartmentalize your entire life at once. Planning an event is a nice way to segue into overall organization.

Invest in supplies. Getting things in order doesn't have to be expensive. Buy a used file cabinet; pick up a box of file folders; install some organizational software on your PC. The money you spend will be well worth the aggravation you save yourself in the end.

Label everything. Have one folder for receipts, another for literature on vendors, another for the guest list, etc. Put a big old label on each file so that you don't accidentally lose your guest list in the recipe file.

Don't compare yourself to others. Your best friend might be the most organized person on the planet; however, the system that works for her may not work for you, so go into this with an open mind. Find your own best methods for keeping information tidy.

A positive attitude is required for those who are striving for order. Do your best to stay on top of things. (Don't let papers pile up until you have to sort them into their various files—something's sure to get lost in the shuffle.) You might just surprise yourself, and you might even find that you enjoy being able to find what you're looking for *when* you're looking for it (and not three months later).

You Need Moxie, Baby

Depending on the size of the party, you may find yourself interviewing various vendors. If you've never been in this position before, and you're not comfortable asking difficult (or even necessary) questions, you might feel a little shy or awkward about the whole thing. Remember this: Vendors deal with potential customers every single day. These customers ask the most off-the-wall, outrageous, beside-the-point questions. They've cleared the path for you already. There is absolutely *nothing* you can ask a vendor that they haven't already been asked. So don't be bashful.

Don't let a banquet manager or restaurant owner or caterer allow you to feel less than intelligent. While it's true that certain businesses make their livings off of weddings and pre-wedding parties (and therefore know an awful lot about them—more than the average bride or MOB), part of their business is (nicely) providing you with all the information you're looking for so that you aren't entering into a blind deal with them. Many wedding-related businesses are excellent in the area of dealing with potential clients; these people know that alienating customers is not in their best interest. It's up to you to have a list of questions and to ask them; nice as these vendors may be, they aren't usually known for their clairvoyance.

Ⓔ ESSENTIAL

When interviewing vendors, remember you're potentially entering into a business deal. That means *you're* paying *them* to provide *you* with a service. Any vendor who isn't willing or able to adequately address your questions and/or concerns is not someone you want to do business with. It's that simple.

Stick to the Plan

Though it's easy to become distracted by the beauty of banquet rooms and the creativity of various caterers, when you're looking for the best vendor(s) for the party you're planning, keep in mind that you *do* have a budget to work with. Yes, the room may be lovely, but what about its price? The menu sounds scrumptious, but is it what you were thinking of in the first place? Keep your guard up just enough to retain a clear picture of the party you were planning before you stepped into the caterer's (or banquet manager's) office and seated yourself in the plush side chair (and were brought coffee by the caterer's assistant).

Stifle Those Comments, Mom

Pretend you're hosting a party. It can be a birthday party, a cocktail party, a dinner party—choose an event. You've booked a restaurant, you've chosen a menu, perhaps you've even researched some icebreaker games. Your plans are working out well until you receive a call from one of your invited guests who tells you that you're doing it all wrong. The location stinks, you should be feeding the guests more than finger foods and cake, and don't even get her going on the topic of the games (she thinks they're tasteless). What would you do? Give her a piece of your mind? Disinvite her?

Now pretend that your daughter's friends or in-laws are planning a pre-wedding party for her and *you're* displeased with the location, the menu, and (you guessed it) the activities. What are you going to do *now*? The right answer: You're going to show up and be a gracious guest.

It's just plain wrong for an invited guest (you, in this instance) to criticize a party. It's worse than wrong—it's rude and crass (*shudder*—two words that should never be associated with the MOB). Bottom line:

If *you're* planning a party, you're free to go in any direction you want with it—just remember that every *other* hostess holds that same privilege. It would be bad enough for the bride to complain about a party that's given in her honor—it's ten times worse for *you* to stick your nose into the matter, proclaiming that your little girl deserves better.

Ⓔ ALERT!

> Being the MOB doesn't mean you're allowed to criticize with immunity. Even though you may be very unhappy with the way another hostess handled your daughter's engagement party or shower, hold your tongue. There's *no way* you can chastise a hostess and come away looking like a decent human.

If your inquiries and comments are your way of saying, "I want to help," try to find a better way to phrase it—such as coming right out and offering to be of assistance to the party planner. If she needs your help, she'll call on you—and if she doesn't, you'll just have to take your seat along with all of the other guests. Even though you are the MOB, you can't force a hostess to accept your help. Attempting to do so usually ends very badly (with you seated at the table furthest from the action).

The Engagement Party

The bride's family has the option of throwing the first engagement party, according to traditional wedding etiquette. You are not in any way obligated to do so, and if you're planning on contributing mightily to the wedding itself, you may feel as though the responsibility of hosting this party should really fall on someone else's shoulders. Whatever position you find yourself in (hostess or guest), you'll need to know what to do, what to wear, and what you'll say when everyone raises their champagne flutes and looks to you.

The Basics

You've decided to follow tradition and toast your daughter and soon-to-be son-in-law. When? Where? In what manner? It's best to plan the engagement party well in advance of other pre-wedding events (such as the bridal shower and bachelorette party) so that it stands on its own for what it is—a happy celebration of the kids' decision to spend eternity together. If the bride and groom are having a long engagement (a year or longer), an engagement party would be appropriate six to eight months before the actual ceremony.

Different hosts have different ideas for engagement parties. Can you go all out and book the fanciest hotel in the city for this event? Sure. But might you also go to the other extreme and clean off the grill for an outdoor patio engagement party? Yep, as long as the bride and groom don't have a serious problem with an ultracasual affair. Keep in mind that the engagement party shouldn't outshine the wedding. If your daughter is planning a simple little ceremony, the engagement party should be scaled down to a similar level of informality.

 FACT

> Hosting an engagement party more than a year before the wedding allows for too much time between the two—and time dilutes *other* people's excitement, lending to a "You're *still* engaged?" attitude. Trying to fit it in too close to the ceremony puts you in danger of competing with pre-wedding parties.

Obviously, the location of the event and the time of day will play a large part in dictating the menu. Most engagement parties tend to swing towards cocktails and hors d'oeuvres, but you can certainly break with that tradition if you have your heart set on a catered meal with all the accoutrements. (Chances are, your guests won't complain if you want to spoil them a bit.) And no matter how formal the party gets, the couple shouldn't expect to be opening gifts by night's end—presents are not given at engagement parties.

The Guest List

Guest lists for an engagement party cause some hostesses a lot of grief. It's best to stick with the old standard rule: Anyone who is invited to a pre-wedding party must also be invited to the wedding. It's just in poor taste to invite a guest to celebrate an upcoming event . . . and then exclude them from that very event.

Some brides and grooms argue that because they're planning a small wedding and they won't be able to invite all of their friends and coworkers to the reception that they *should* invite them to the engagement party. The theory goes that this is the bride and groom's way of making sure the noninvitees are somehow included in the overall excitement of the wedding season. However . . . guests are bound to question *why* the bride and groom are having a small wedding. Is it a matter of cost? (Where did the money for the engagement party come from, then, and why isn't it being applied toward the cost of a larger reception that everyone could be invited to?) Is it a matter of privacy? And if so, why are they inviting people to join them in merriment *now*?

Ⓔ ESSENTIAL

Don't offend friends and/or relatives by inviting them to pre-wedding parties when they won't be invited to the wedding. If the bride and groom are hosting their own engagement party, you probably can't stop errant invitations. If *you're* the hostess, though, the guest list is largely your responsibility.

Put yourself in the position of these guests of convenience: Would you want to attend a party to honor people who weren't going to somehow squeeze you into the major festivities? You'd probably feel hurt (and used) when you learned that you weren't important enough to the engaged couple to make the final cut.

ⓔ FACT

You'll need the perfect outfit for the engagement party, of course. The formality, time of day, and season all play a part in what you'll wear. For a formal affair, a dress or dressy pantsuit is appropriate. For a less formal party, a casual dress, a skirt, or pants are all fine.

Be Their Guest

If someone else, the groom's family or the bride's friends or the bride and groom themselves, decides to host the engagement party, what are you expected to do? Well . . . you're expected to show up and to be good company. You're expected to lend a hand if and when you're needed to—*without* crossing into controlling territory, which means you'll attend the party with an *on-call* attitude. You won't be involved in the planning, and you won't be responsible for the execution of the party, but because you *are* the MOB, you really should keep an eye out for any trouble spots. Is the host having trouble greeting guests *and* hanging their coats? Grab some hangers and help out. Are some of the guests looking for napkins and having no luck? Pop into the kitchen and grab a stack.

It's easy to fall into the trap of doing so much that the host actually gets offended—as though you're trying to take over a party that you're not sponsoring—so when in doubt, *ask*. Being helpful is a wonderful trait in an MOB, and few folks would refuse the assistance—but some will.

The Bride's Showers

Pick up any bridal etiquette book, and you'll learn that the MOB is supposed to keep her nose out of the bridal shower. That's great news for you if your daughter's brides-maids are well versed in the etiquette of showers, *and* responsible enough *and* financially stable enough to plan a shower for her. Occasionally, however, especially in the case of the younger bride (and her college-aged brides-maids), the shower sits there, like a wallflower, waiting to be acknowledged. Are you allowed to save the day?

Get Going, Girls!

Younger bridesmaids (or those who haven't read the bridal books) may not have any clue that they're sup-posed to be planning a shower for their friend. Is it all right for you to give them a nudge in the right direction? A very *limited* nudge is all you're entitled to—and it should be directed towards the maid of honor, since she's sup-posed to be taking charge of this particular event. A nice way to find out whether she has anything planned is to simply ask: "Have you girls thought about the shower? Is there anything I can do to help?" You'll be able to gauge from her response whether a party is in the works—or this is the first she's heard (and/or thought) of it.

Ⓔ ALERT!

Since showers are ideally held about two months prior to the wedding, you'll want to know the game plan at least four months before the ceremony—so that if the bridesmaids *are* delinquent in their responsibilities, you can step in and whip something up yourself.

Something else to consider: Has your daughter stood up in any of her bridesmaids' weddings? Did *she* contribute to the planning and the cost of *their* showers? If not, you can be sure that at least one of the bridesmaids is wondering why she's being held responsible for the very same duty your daughter neglected during *her* engagement.

Mom to the Rescue

If the bridesmaids *have* neglected their duties, you don't need to list their names as hostesses on the shower invitations. Since many MOBs do host bridal showers these days, go ahead and put your own name on that line, or choose another relative or friend to be the figurehead for the day.

Are you entitled to demand a financial contribution from the bridesmaids for a shower that you're planning? Not really. Even though the girls *should* have made the plans themselves, you can't insist that they pitch in on particulars that were completely of your choosing. The place you've chosen might be out of their price range—and they may have hesitated with the planning in the first place because they're all broke. You can certainly request that they pitch in on the party, but you can't place a lien on their bank accounts if they fail to do so.

If you do decide to take the reins of planning this event, or at least want to help organize it, you'll need to know what showers are like these days, and how to make your daughter's both memorable and enjoyable. The following sections will give you some planning pointers.

Dish It Out

What will you feed the ladies who attend the shower? Most often, showers are afternoon events and include light fare, such as buffets with various salads and deli trays. You can also host a sit-down lunch. Just be aware that most guests will expect to eat something substantial, and since the vast majority of them will be lugging a gift for the bride along with them, you want to make sure they feel welcome and well taken care of for the afternoon.

Showers can be held in a banquet hall or restaurant or in someone's home. If you're inviting seventy-five women, really consider whether you're up to the task of setting up tables and chairs and cooking for such a large group. It's definitely easier on your back to hold a large party in a restaurant or banquet facility. If you're renting chairs, tables, linens, and a tent (and glasses . . . and silverware) for a backyard party, it might actually be *less* expensive to just move the party elsewhere. If you have loads of helpers, though, as well as plenty of room and folding tables stored in your basement, a party at home might just be a viable option.

E FACT

There's no need to order formal invitations for the bridal shower. Any stationery store will have pretty shower invitations that can be hand-printed by you and your little helpers. Just make sure anyone who's being invited to the shower is also going to be invited to the wedding.

For a large, at-home party, you might want to look into hiring a caterer, unless you and your family love the idea of cooking for the masses. Just make sure before you commit to all of this work that your assistants are *as* committed. You're amazing, all right, but you are one woman with one set of hands. You can't do *everything*.

You'll need to make sure the ladies have plenty to drink. If you're offering wine and cocktails to your guests, make sure they're given a choice of nonalcoholic drinks, as well. If you're hosting a party at home, make sure you've stocked the bar with lemons, limes, celery, olives—anything that your guests will need for their drinks.

Ⓔ ESSENTIAL

Don't forget about dessert! Wherever ladies gather to celebrate an upcoming wedding, it's only natural that someone will be looking for sweets. Shower cakes are traditional in some parts of the country, while in other areas, anything goes—and usually goes fast!

Play Along

There are two schools of thought on shower games: Ladies either love 'em or hate 'em. There's no middle ground. Regardless of *your* personal feelings, take a look at your guest list and ask yourself which guests will be expecting to compete with the other ladies for a prize. Like it or not, members of the older generation (and even some members of the younger generations) might well be expecting to play a game or two—that's what ladies *do* at showers, as far as they're concerned.

There are some safe standards that almost every guest will tolerate (such as "Guess How Many Heart Candies Are in the Jar"), and *then* there are games that might only serve to divide your guests into two camps: those who will play, and those who won't. (The opposing groups will eye each other suspiciously for the rest of the afternoon.) These are usually group activities (something along the lines of each table being forced to compose a single poem about the bride and groom). If the guests don't know each other extremely well, your well-intentioned attempt at trying to *make* them get to know each other could backfire. Unless you and the bride really, *really* love shower games, try to keep them simple and as humiliation-free for the guests as possible.

We Have a Winner!

Offer prizes for the winners and favors (or door prizes) for *all* of your guests—and have plenty on hand in case there's a dispute and you end up with double or triple winners somewhere along the line. When you're purchasing these items, think about buying something either perishable or practical—and avoid choosing prizes that will end up in someone's junk drawer or in the trash. Ideas for favors and prizes include heart- or flower-shaped soaps, sachets, small houseplants, heart-shaped chocolates (the best quality), nice pens, notepads, small silver or porcelain frames, and bath oils or salts.

There are many, many other options and ideas for games and prizes. One last word of caution, though: Think twice before you personalize these items with the bride and/or groom's names. Your guests are more likely to use (and appreciate) something that they feel is *theirs*—and they won't if your daughter's name is all over those otherwise lovely little notepads and frames you've purchased as door prizes.

Ⓔ FACT

Coed showers are gaining in popularity. This is a nice idea for a couple of reasons: For one thing, a coed shower gets *everyone* together before the wedding, and for another thing, the couple will need some practical items (such as tools) which rarely find their way onto a bridal registry.

Theme Showers

Who *doesn't* love a good theme party? The possibilities for shower themes are endless, because a bride-to-be usually needs just about everything for her new home and her new life. Some guests really love theme parties, because they *know* what they're shopping for—it actually might make their work a little easier. Consider these gift-giving themes:

- Kitchen
- Lingerie
- Pottery
- Recipe or cooking exchange
- Gift baskets

Some of these titles are self-explanatory; others aren't. At a basket shower, for example, each guest gives the bride an entire basket with its own theme—someone might give her a basket filled with cleaning items, for example, while someone else might hand her a basket filled with the ingredients for an entire meal. The guests can get as creative as they want, and the bride will end up with a house full of useful supplies.

Theme showers can take off in any direction. If the newlyweds will be entertaining frequently in their new home, a stock-the-bar shower might be a great idea for them: Each guest brings a bottle for the newlyweds' liquor cabinet. (Any couple who has ever had to stock their own bar knows that this expense adds up quickly, especially if you're starting from scratch.)

Bridesmaids' Luncheon

Technically, the bride is supposed to take charge of this gathering—however, since you're supposed to be helping the bride, you might find yourself lending a hand. The bridesmaids' luncheon is strictly optional—if several of the bridesmaids are coming from out of town, and there's no way to coordinate everyone's schedules *before* the day of the wedding (or rehearsal), it's probably best to just skip it. Trying to squeeze a luncheon in on the day of the ceremony will defeat the purpose of this gathering. It's supposed to be a nice, relaxing afternoon for the bride and her girlfriends.

Since this is a *thank you* from the bride to her attendants, each of them should be included, obviously. Some brides also invite the moms (and if *you're* invited, the groom's mom really should be, too), and, depending on the time and location of the get-together, may invite the flower girl (whose own mother should also be in attendance). This is an intimate get-together, so the guest list shouldn't read like a phone book.

Ⓔ ESSENTIAL

This get-together doesn't *have* to be lunch. The bride can turn it into a bridesmaids' dinner, a night on the town, a day at the spa, or a movie marathon night at the bride's home.

Saying Thanks

The bridesmaids' luncheon is the bride's way of showing her appreciation for the hard work her bridesmaids have done. At the very least, they've spent quite a bit of money on their ensembles for the wedding, but they also should have paid for the shower, a shower and wedding gift for the bride, and their personal travel expenses, if any. That's a lot to ask from a girlfriend, and even though the attendants knew what they were getting into when they accepted a role in the wedding party, they'll appreciate your daughter's acknowledgement of their efforts.

On the other hand, a bride will occasionally find herself saddled with unruly and unpleasant bridesmaids who are bound and determined to give her nothing but grief. In this case, should she still thank them by hosting a lunch in their honor? Let common sense prevail.

Luncheon Traditions

This event is a great time for the bride to give her attendants the gifts she's chosen for them. The bridesmaids' luncheon also traditionally includes a cake with some symbolic meaning baked right in. In the first variation, the bridesmaids dig into a pink cake that includes some sort of trinket—a coin, a ring, or a thimble are common. The lucky lady who finds the trinket in her slice of cake is the next to walk down the aisle. Another take on the cake comes from Victorian England. The cake is placed on top of charms, which are attached to ribbons that are long enough to hang off the cake plate. Each bridesmaid pulls a ribbon to reveal her charm at the other end. The bride can choose the charms herself (available where wedding supplies are sold), and attach meaning to them in her own creative way.

Speech Time

Hosts or hostesses of pre-wedding parties are often called upon to offer up some kind words regarding the engagement. The bride's dad may jump at this idea, or you may be the one who has a thing or two to say . . . but what?

If you don't speak in public on a regular basis, and if, in fact, the thought of holding the attention of a roomful of people gives you the willies, you might give up on the idea of offering a toast before you've given it enough thought. This is your daughter's engagement, after all, and folks will be looking to you, especially if you're the hostess, to lend your official seal of approval (in the form of *words*) to the union.

If you do decide to voice your endorsement, plan what you want to say. Nothing's more painful for guests to watch than a speaker who's trying—and failing—to hold the floor. Give yourself plenty of time to jot down your ideas and to express them appropriately. Practice at least once or twice—and yes, do it in front of the mirror. You want to get a feel for your facial expressions, as well. If you keep it short and simple, you're sure to make the kind of impression you're shooting for.

Chapter 5

Dressing the Part

So much to consider! You'll need to figure out what to wear to the pre-wedding parties (which is not always as easy as it should be), and you'll have to make sure your husband isn't attempting to break out his tux from college. The bride is begging you to help her find her ensemble—and meanwhile, the bridesmaids are in a lather over the dress your daughter has chosen for *them*. It's just part of the territory for the MOB.

Simple Rules for Yourself

If you're starting to feel as though there are no longer any hard and fast rules to stick to as far as weddings and pre-wedding events are concerned, you're not far off the mark. If you're a woman who *craves* order and needs instructions (as specific as possible, please) in order to feel comfortable in these situations, you might be feeling a little unsure of yourself. Don't sweat it. There's very little chance of your showing up to a wedding event dressed inappropriately . . . as long as you stick to a certain set of rules.

 FACT

Not all events provide guests with strict dress codes. Not to worry. Just keep in mind that you're celebrating an upcoming wedding, and dress for the dignity of the occasion. In other words, it's better to err on the side of caution and go a little dressier than to be too casual.

Rule One: Dress in Layers

Especially where the pre-wedding parties are concerned, you may have no idea what you're walking into. Is a party on the patio of the tennis club a formal event, or an informal one? Does a dinner at the groom's parents' house call for shorts or a dress? You can always call the host and ask, of course, which is often the easiest and most obvious way to alleviate your fears—but if you're just not comfortable making that call, you can *still* show up dressed correctly and pretend you knew all along what everyone else would be wearing.

The secret? No, it's not throwing an outfit for any occasion in the trunk of your car—it's as simple as *layering*. Not sure if this is a semicasual or semidressy event? Choose a nice dress or a semidressy pair of pants, throw a nice jacket on top of it, and voilà! You're dressed for both parties. Remove the jacket if the party is more on the casual side.

Rule Two: Read the Invitation

Of course, any party that is *really* formal will say so on the invitation. White tie (also sometimes called "Ultraformal") is the dressiest of all events, and requires a full-length gown for women. Men should wear a tux with a white tie, vest and shirt. Black tie ("Formal") gives you more choices—you can wear a long dress, a cocktail dress, or separates that are dressy enough for the occasion. Men are expected to wear tuxedos. Of course, not every invitation will be so easily deciphered. What does "Creative Black Tie" mean? And how about "Black Tie Optional"? Are these people just out to confuse and frustrate you? If they are, they'll fail—because you have your handy list of dress definitions:

Cocktail Attire: You'll wear a dressy dress on the shorter side (knee length or just below). Men wear suits.

Dress Casual: Think business casual on a more formal scale.

Black Tie Optional/Black Tie Invited: Same as Black Tie (for women, at least). Men can wear tuxes or dark suits.

Creative Black Tie: Just what it sounds like—an event that gives men and women room to experiment with newer dressy looks. (Men are limited to stylish tuxes.)

Follow your instincts (and your glossary), and you'll show up looking like a million bucks.

Rule Three: Keep Tabs on Your Spouse

As if dressing yourself weren't hard enough, there's your husband, attempting to shimmy his way into a suit he hasn't worn in ten years. (He's planning on wearing this to your daughter's engagement party, by the way.) Before your hair turns white from the shock of such a sight, have a little talk with him. If he has never had a clue as to how to dress himself, *help him*. You can't show up looking like a movie star being accompanied by a specimen who is apparently trapped in some sort of time warp that has also served to shrink his clothes.

Yes, some dads are eccentric, and yes, everyone may *know* that the bride's dad is known for his fashion missteps (or, more correctly, his rather intellectual *disdain* for fashion), but for any wedding-related event, he should look his best and be dressed appropriately.

Rule Four: Don't Upstage the Bride . . . *Ever*

MOBs often find themselves torn between wearing an absolutely smashing dress that comes very close to calling a lot of attention to themselves (which, of course, is what this particular dress is all about) and respecting the rule that states that the bride should be the prettiest woman at the wedding. Is it right that you should be condemned to don a lesser frock just so that your daughter won't be upset?

Oh, Mom . . . you know that it *is* fair, and that you shouldn't outdo the bride on her wedding day or at any of her pre-wedding parties. Yes, you look great in that dress you're dying to wear—but you'll look just as good in something more subdued (even if you hate and regularly rebel against that word).

(E) QUESTION

What type of dress should a mother of the bride avoid?

Stay away from any dress in neon colors or animal prints, a dress that shows an awful lot of cleavage, or anything that shows your great thighs in their entirety. This goes for the wedding and any pre-wedding parties.

The Perfect Dress—Where *Is* It?

Some women love shopping; others abhor the practice. If you fall into the former group, finding a dress for the wedding will be a piece of cake (or at least you'll have a blast looking); if you fall into the latter group, you may be putting off this task until the very last minute.

Start Early

Dresses for weddings (including the bride's dress, the attendants' dresses, and dresses for the moms) don't change all that drastically from one year to the next. Sure, you'll want something that's appropriate to the time of year, but unless you have to be on the cutting edge of what's hot *right now* in the fashion world, chances are, a dress from last year will suit you fine—and you might even find yourself a real bargain in the process. Allowing yourself plenty of time for this project also means that you'll be able to check out dresses all over town, in bridal shops, in department stores, and in boutiques.

 FACT

Shopping can really tire some people out. Take care of yourself before and after you go on the hunt for your MOB dress. Get a good night's sleep, take a break when you're feeling weary, and don't shop when you're in a bad mood.

Another reason you should start looking for your dress as soon as the bride has set the wedding date is so that you have time to try different styles and colors and find out what looks best on you. If you leave finding your dress until a month before the wedding, you'll choose whatever's available—and *not* what flatters your shape and skin tone. You will be on display at the wedding, so you want to look your absolute best.

Ⓔ ESSENTIAL

In choosing a dress, try to go for a subtle shade and a classic style. Perhaps asymmetrical dresses are all the rage now—but ten years from now, pictures of your dress will elicit roars of laughter from your loved ones.

Defining the Perfect Dress

What are you looking for, exactly? Something that blends with the bride's chosen colors. Most moms use the bridesmaids' dresses as a palette. If their gowns are green, you shouldn't choose a pink dress. A different shade of green or even a dress in a complimentary shade of blue would be a better choice. You want to avoid white, ivory, black, red, anything too bright (like, say, an electric blue gown), and anything too overdone. (A matching feather boa, for example, might be a little much.)

Although black is becoming more acceptable for MOBs and guests alike to wear to weddings, ask yourself whether you want to be under scrutiny for the color of your dress (no matter how progressive the fashion world is becoming, MOBs who wear black are always suspected of harboring some ill will towards the union), or if you'd rather have guests compliment you for how you look in a particular dress.

Save Your Sanity

Go to lunch. Go to dinner. Make a day (or two, or twenty) of it. If you're hitting a lot of shops and you fear you won't remember where you saw which dress, take a notebook along and write down a description of each dress alongside the address of the store. Knowing that she tried on the perfect dress *somewhere*—but she can't remember *where*—is enough to make an MOB decide to wear capris and flip-flops to the reception.

If you know anyone who has recently played the role of MOB, ask her about her dress-shopping experience. She might be able to steer you in the right direction—or away from a less than terrific shop—and save you some time in the process.

Take a friend along for the ride so that you can also get an honest assessment of how the dress looks on you from someone who doesn't stand to make a commission from the sale. You'll want someone to tell you if the dress you love from the front is less-than-flattering from the rear, and you'll also want a truthful opinion of the style and color—so make sure your shopping companion is an honest woman.

Frugality Is a Virtue (Isn't It?)

Maybe you walk into the first dress shop on your list and you find it—*the* dress, the one you were imagining, the one that makes you look twenty pounds slimmer and ten years younger. One problem: It costs twice as much as you wanted to spend. Oh, but it's worth it, isn't it? You are the MOB, and you do have to look your best.

ⓔ ALERT!

> If you're even considering spending far more than you originally planned on a certain dress, take a day or two to consider your decision. You may decide that it's worth it, or that the dress made you temporarily lose your mind—but you'll be less likely to suffer buyer's remorse.

This is very true, but you don't have to spend way too much to look great. Know what you're willing to spend before you walk through the doors of a dress shop and stick with that figure. Spending a *little* more when you find the perfect dress is all right—but blowing your budget entirely isn't wise, unless it's a dress that you really, truly can wear again—and again, and again.

But before you make yourself *that* promise (the same promise made by one-time dress wearers all over the world, by the way) ask yourself *where* you'll wear it.

If there's another wedding coming up in your family, chances are you'll end up buying a new dress for that event (because your *kids* don't want you wearing the same dress to both weddings). If it's a very formal dress, and you're planning on wearing it to the many formal events you'll be attending in the next year, make sure you won't be seeing the same crowd at those gatherings, or they'll wonder whether you wear that dress to bed, too.

If you'll be attending several weddings and several formal events (and you're 100 percent positive that this dress isn't going to scream "mother of the bride approaching!" and you won't be seeing the same people at each affair), then perhaps it's wise to invest a little more in a dress. Otherwise, resign yourself to the fact that you will most likely wear this dress once, and don't go completely overboard price-wise.

Seamstresses Versus Bridal Shops

If you can't find what you're looking for in a shop, or if you have found exactly what you want, but you're not willing to pay the bridal shop's prices, you might look into hiring a seamstress to create your one-of-a-kind MOB dress. Still, you're unsure about handing over the duties to one woman; the dress shop at least has other dresses on the premises in case disaster strikes. Is dealing with one safer than the other? Not really. There are pros and cons to seamstresses and dress shops.

Ask anyone who knows a great seamstress: She's worth every cent she'll charge you for her labor if you just can't buy clothes off the rack, or if you can't find anything suitable—as long as the two of you can communicate effectively. This means that you have to be willing to spell out exactly what you want without being overly demanding and unrealistic. She'll tell you if she's not capable of producing the dress you're asking for in the time frame you're giving her—but it may well be that *no one* (at least no human) can whip up a hand-beaded, full-length gown in a week's time.

 FACT

> Be very careful when you choose a seamstress; if something happens, and your dress is not completed as promised, you might find yourself running to the mall or to a dress shop anyway—and you'll have to haggle with the seamstress for a refund.

A good seamstress usually has her hands full—you're probably not her one and only client, and she only has the one set of hands and a given number of hours in any one day to work with. Give your seamstress a call at least six to eight months prior to the wedding—even sooner if you know she's in high demand.

The advantage to patronizing a dress shop, of course, is that you can try on the dresses and get an idea of how each one looks before you buy one. (No such luck with a seamstress.) Most bridal shops and high-end dress shops have tailors who will make sure that your dress fits as it should. You'll pay extra for this service, of course. The disadvantage of buying off the rack is that the dresses in these shops can be very expensive, and you're limited to their selection.

(E) ESSENTIAL

Keep in mind, clueing the groom's mom into the particulars of your dress isn't the same thing as dictating to her what to wear. She *should* choose a dress that's suitable to the level of formality of the wedding and something that also complements your dress.

"Hello, My Dress Is Pink."

Yes, you're supposed to call the groom's mom and let her in on all of the exciting news of your dress-shopping extravaganza so that she can choose her dress . . . and so that she doesn't choose the *same* dress. (Horrors!) This is another good reason for you to get started early, because tradition states that the groom's mother has to wait for you to make your selection before she can make hers. She'll start getting pretty irritated if you've put the dress shopping off until three weeks before the wedding. That irritation might just spill over into an ugly MOB vs. MOG confrontation, which can be avoided altogether if you simply get on the ball and pick out your dress at least two months prior to the ceremony.

The Bride's Dress

Aside from choosing your own dress for the ceremony, there will be the small matter of the bride finding her gown. Depending on your relationship with your daughter, you may be called upon to assist her in the hunt, or she may not want you within a two-mile radius of the dress shop she's visiting. (Believe it or not, some moms and daughters have a very hard time shopping together. Add the stress of a wedding to this situation, and a bride may honestly fear that she and her mother won't be speaking to each other at the end of a very long shopping day.)

If she does want your help, and you do tend to be a bit excitable or your comments tend to be very blunt, try to cool your heels a bit and remember that the bride is probably more emotional than usual right now. She's embarking on the hunt for the dress she's dreamed of since she was a little girl. Be *very* careful with your comments.

Shops or Warehouses?

A bride who is looking for a traditional, big white gown will often begin her search in a bridal shop. Most of these stores require appointments. The dresses are large and unwieldy, and an employee of the store will be dispatched to carry the gowns from the rack to the dressing room, and to assist the bride as she tries on dress after dress after dress. Bottom line: Plan ahead, and don't expect to be welcomed with open arms if you're popping in off the street.

Of course, these days, a bride can alternatively head to a bridal warehouse or even shop online for her dress. Is it wise to patronize these businesses? After all, a bride can save herself a bundle—but what are the risks?

(E) ALERT!

Warehouse dresses may be damaged. The bride needs to carefully inspect any dress she's considering for loose threads, tears, missing beads, stains, and the like. She should also get the store's policy on returns *in writing* before she takes her dress out of the store.

If a bride can tolerate the no-frills atmosphere of a warehouse setting, she might just walk away with a bargain. There will be no plush dressing room, no beverages, no store employees catering to her needs. She'll have to hunt through the racks herself to find the perfect dress. However, before your daughter gets too excited by the amount of money she's saving by foregoing the personal service, you should advise her that when she buys a dress from a warehouse, she will be responsible for finding a seamstress for any alterations and/or repairs, an expense that may just defeat the purpose of buying off the rack.

Buying online comes with its own set of worries. Most online bridal shops (and auctions) do not allow returns, and since it's impossible to try a dress on in cyberspace, purchasing a gown this way is *very* risky. Even if your daughter knows the exact dress she's looking for, she's better off giving her business—and her money—to a local shop. If something goes wrong with the order or the dress, it will be *much* easier for her to get her point across (i.e., someone had better fix the problem quickly or risk the wrath of the bride) when she's dealing with a real live person standing in front of her in a dress shop instead of a Web site.

Make a Game Plan

Shopping for a bride's gown can be an exhausting, head-spinning experience. Unless she finds the dress she's looking for on your first day out, you may find that all of the frocks she's trying on are starting to look very similar. Where once you could differentiate between a quality gown and a cheap one, you're having trouble seeing past the tulle and the beads . . . and you're leaning towards a dress you suspect you might hate.

How might you avoid shopping overload and confusion before it starts? By sitting down with your daughter before you visit your first bridal shop and discussing what she wants versus what might not work. For example, if your daughter is very pale, pure white may not be the right color for her. She might look best in an off-white dress, or something with a little color added to it. The hottest style may not be the best pick for her shape—and there are far too many brides out there who go for the current trend instead of considering what looks best on them.

Ⓔ ALERT!

There is a right way to tell your daughter that a dress doesn't look good on her ("Honey, I think that this other style is very slimming, and this dress you have on isn't.") and a wrong way ("That dress makes your butt look even bigger than it is. Now put on the other one.").

Look Away!

So you've put your time in, schlepping from shop to shop, discussing the merits of silk versus chiffon, debating whether white or eggshell is a better color on her, oohing and ahhing over the best gowns—and your daughter has chosen the most unflattering dress she tried on. And she *loves* it. What are you supposed to do now? Take a week off from shopping so that both of you can mull things over. When you return to the shop, she may notice the obvious flaws in her decision.

If it's a matter of style—the dress makes her look very heavy, for example, or it makes her look gaunt, or the color just drains the life from her cheeks—these are things you're right to point out to her. They will show in the wedding pictures, and she'll realize too late that this dress didn't suit her at all.

If, on the other hand, this is just a difference of taste (yours versus hers), you need to hold your tongue. You might hate all the beading on the dress she's chosen, or you might have an objection to the length of the train. As long as the gown she's chosen doesn't look horrible *on* her (there's a *very* fine line here, and you may have to overcome your personal aversion to certain fabrics or styles), there's no valid reason for her not to wear it to her wedding. You may state your opinion once—*nicely*—then drop it.

Time to Accessorize!

She'll also be shopping for a headpiece and/or veil, and she really should try these on with her gown. Headpieces are meant to accentuate the gown—*not* vice versa. If she's chosen a very plain gown, her headpiece shouldn't weigh ten pounds and be covered with reflective discs. The only way to be absolutely sure that the headpiece and gown will compliment each other is to shop for them simultaneously.

Buyer Be *Very* Wary

You may have heard that some bridal shops run scams on their customers. How can you protect yourself (and your daughter) from falling prey to these nefarious shopkeepers? Your first line of defense is to get a personal recommendation from a friend or acquaintance who has dealt with this particular business *recently* (you want to know that you're not dealing with new management and new store policies). Take that recommendation with a grain of salt: Though your friend might have had a wonderful relationship with this store, her experience doesn't guarantee that you'll come away without a single complaint.

Has She Grown *That* Much?

The most common bridal shop scam out there involves excessive alterations. Many bridal shops make *a lot* of money from tailoring dresses—and the more alterations that need to be done on a certain dress, the more money in the cash register.

Make sure that when your daughter tries on a dress, it has a dress-size tag in it. Some shops remove these tags to prevent brides from gleaning any pertinent information from them (such as the size, the designer, the style number). How is this a scam? Let's say your daughter wears a size ten dress. She slips on the floor model of a gown that seems to fit perfectly, but there's no tag to indicate what size she has on—so a shop employee can tell her that the dress she's currently wearing is a size fourteen, and this particular line of dresses tends to run small. Your daughter orders the dress in a fourteen, thinking it will fit like a dream, only to find when it arrives—surprise, surprise—that it's hanging off of her, and she'll need extensive alterations to make it fit the way it should. *Cha-ching*!

Alterations on a wedding gown are not *always* a scam, and are actually often necessary. In addition, many gowns really *do* run smaller than the average off-the-rack, everyday dress. When the tag is missing from the sample dress, though, you should be suspicious (because you have no way to tell what size it *really* is, and you're trusting an employee whom you don't know to be truthful).

Ⓔ **ALERT!**

Bridal shops battle each other for customers, which is one reason tags are sometimes removed from dresses. Shop A certainly doesn't want to make it easy for your daughter to compare the price of the same dress at Shop B. (Removing tags from new garments is *illegal*, by the way.)

More Shop Shams

Other things to watch for and avoid when doing business with a dress shop:

Don't allow the dress to be shipped to your home. You want the *shop* to be ultimately responsible for securing the bride's dress; you and your daughter have enough to worry about.

Don't put more than 50 percent down at the time the dress is ordered. Even for special orders, reputable stores will not require more than half of the full payment.

Don't pay deposits in cash. Again, no reputable store will demand cash payment. Using your credit card is your safest bet.

Read the contract. Make sure everything is spelled out—the price, the size of the dress, the manufacturer or designer, the order date, the delivery date, any extra charges or discounts, and any special instructions (e.g., long sleeves instead of short).

Ⓔ FACT

Of course, your daughter may choose to have her dress made. She should contact the seamstress as soon as she makes this decision. A simple gown might only take a couple of months to sew, but a more complex one (read: neck-to-hem beads) might take a minimum of six months.

Rest assured, most bridal shops are on the up-and-up, but it's important to have a little knowledge of the darker side of the business so that you and your daughter don't end up with horrible memories of this experience. Before plunking down money for your daughter's wedding dress, check the Better Business Bureau's Web site to see if there are any complaints against the shop you're considering doing business with.

Bridesmaids' Garb

Surely, you're not expected to pick out the bridesmaids' dresses. You're right—this duty belongs to the bride. But you can help her make a choice that won't alienate every single one of her attendants. What are the most common complaints bridesmaids have about their dresses?

Cost. If most of the girls are also incurring travel expenses for the wedding, or if all of them are in college and broke, encourage your daughter to choose a reasonably priced dress.

Color. There are just some colors that are difficult for most people to wear. Orange. Certain shades of yellow. Neon pink. Urge the bride to choose a classic (*not* trendy) hue that will flatter her bridesmaids.

Cut. Overweight bridesmaids do not appreciate having to spatula themselves into a sheath. No bridesmaid enjoys a dress cut down to her bellybutton—especially in church.

Comfort. Some fabrics are more comfortable than others. Since these girls will be spending the day in their dresses, posing for picture after picture, the bride will want them to look happy—and not itchy.

If your daughter is shopping with an attendant or two, you may not see the dresses until they've been ordered. She's a big girl, and she can make this decision on her own—she may not want or need your help. This is another area where diplomacy is extremely important. Say too much, and she may shut you out completely; say nothing at all, and her bridesmaids may be forced to stage a mutiny.

If she's gone off the deep end, and is looking at $500 dresses for bridesmaids who have only recently moved out of the sorority house (and are crammed into tiny apartments or living with their parents for financial reasons), appeal to her sense of fair play. Yes, she wants them to look beautiful at her wedding—but she's also asking them to spend their own money on these garments. She should try to meet them in the middle and choose comfortable, reasonably priced dresses.

Chapter 6

Communications 101

Isn't planning the wedding supposed to be fun, fun, fun? How come you're in the middle of a whole bunch of people who seem to be a little crabby? Your daughter is kind of going off the deep end, her future husband has sure changed his stripes, and the groom's family is up to something—you just feel it. Can you learn to communicate effectively with all of these folks without losing your own grip on reality—and before things turn really ugly?

Is It Worth a Fight?

Some issues are worth a fight . . . and some just aren't. That's the number one thing you have to remember as you move forward in the wedding planning. No matter who's giving you a hard time—the bride, the groom, his parents—you have to decide whether the issue at hand is really worth your time. You're expending a lot of energy planning this wedding, and it's easy to get riled up over every little potential mishap or disagreement. You simply can't afford to burn out early in the game— and you certainly need your wits about you as the wedding approaches.

Worth It

To determine what is worth arguing over, and who is worth arguing with, you have to determine your priorities, some of which will most likely correspond with your top budgeting picks. Keep in mind, if you're the one paying for most of this wedding, you have much more leverage and are more entitled to voice your opinion on matters of great concern to you. This *doesn't* mean, however, that you are given free reign to disregard the bride's opinions (or those of the groom). It means that you are going to have to work that much harder to reach a happy compromise.

In a nutshell, anything that is going to affect your pocketbook and/or your guests adversely is worth getting into with the bride, the groom, or whomever. If you're spending a lot of money on the reception food, for example, you obviously have a vested interest in ensuring that the eats are appropriate to the occasion and are actually something that your guests will *want* to ingest. If your daughter is insisting on a completely vegetarian buffet, complete with tofu and bean sprouts, you'll want to remind her that not everyone is vegetarian, and that many guests will be expecting some sort of meat. She may not see your point, but you're right on the money, and this *is* something that's worthy of a tussle.

Ⓔ FACT

Your ultimate goal in any wedding debate is working out a compromise. You don't have to have everything done completely your way, and neither does the bride (though she may not realize this yet). If you're willing to give a little in some areas, chances are, she'll give a little in others.

Not Worth It

Anything that doesn't affect you or your guests directly is simply not worth your aggravation. The bride is insisting on having ten bridesmaids? Hey, it's her wedding. You're not shelling out for their dresses. The groom is planning on wearing tuxedo shorts to the reception? This is a borderline call, of course, because you're planning a lovely reception and, in your opinion, those shorts are tacky. But he is an adult, presumably, and this is his wedding, too. He's not actually costing you any money, he's probably not going to ruin the day for the guests, and no one is going to judge you for your son-in-law's error in fashion judgment.

There will undoubtedly be some gray areas of concern—the groom wants to sing a song at the reception, or the groom's mother wants to wear a dress to the wedding that's all wrong for the occasion. Remember, you can't control everything—and you shouldn't try. You're not all-powerful; you're human. Try as you might, you can't prevent every possible mishap or error in judgment. Learn to roll with some things, or you'll end up being miserable on the happiest day of your daughter's life.

Ⓔ ESSENTIAL

Keeping yourself sane is the name of the game. If you don't allow yourself to be drawn into situations that, in the end, mean very little, you'll have a much better chance of actually making it to the wedding . . . instead of being locked in a little rubber room.

The Emotional Bride

Oh, daughters can be such a joy—when they aren't on the warpath or having a nervous breakdown, that is. As happy as a bride-to-be is supposed to feel, some engaged women find that the stress of planning the wedding and preparing for an entirely new life takes its toll on their emotional state. Your previously sunny girl may turn into someone you hardly recognize, and everyone around her may start to wonder why she's so shaky when she's about to get everything she's ever wanted (the perfect man and a sweet life with him). Though you may find her personality change disturbing, it's actually quite common—and thankfully temporary—among many brides.

She's on Overload

In this era of career women, it's not uncommon for a new bride-to-be to find that there simply aren't enough hours in the day for her to get her work done, call the florist, have dinner with her Sweetie, show up for an appointment with the dressmaker, and do the laundry. Today's women are busy little bees—often, they're juggling full-time work with personal relationships and their own homes. Throw a wedding into her appointment book and she may feel as though she doesn't have time to do anything as well as she would like—or that *something* is simply not going to get done. If the bride is paying for a big portion of her wedding, she may also be worrying about her dwindling bank account, and whether it's wise to spend so much on a wedding. On the other hand, if she and the groom have opted for a smaller ceremony for monetary reasons, she may be feeling a bit sad over not having the grand wedding of her childhood dreams.

What can you do for an overly stressed bride? Offer your help, and don't rush to judge her state of mind.

(In other words, don't compound her emotional state by reminding her that this is supposed to be the happiest time of her whole entire life. She will not appreciate this suggestion, and chances are, it will only add to her stress.) Support her and stand by her.

You're a Little Scared of Her

It's sort of funny to imagine a bride who thinks of herself as some sort of engaged princess—it's not so funny, though, if she happens to be your daughter, and she isn't about to allow you to be the queen in this scenario. No, she's the only member of the Royal Family, and you'll all have to just accept that. Not only are *you* tired of this attitude, but your entire family is avoiding her, and you suspect her future in-laws are none too happy about this new side of her personality, either. Do you ignore it, do you address it, or do you just stay as far away from her as possible?

Obviously, an engagement ring does not grant her the right to treat others badly. *You* know that being engaged does not catapult her into some strange celebrity existence, and *you* know that it's only a matter of time before she comes back down to earth. Getting these messages through to her will be a hard sell, but it may be worth a try, especially if her behavior is truly out of bounds (beyond annoying and veering into mean territory).

One problem you're going to run into when trying to correct the bad Princess Bride: She probably won't hear you. She might even take every valid point you make and try to turn it into an attack on her character. Don't give in, and don't be drawn into a bigger fight. Get your point across and then let it go. You've done all you can at that point. As childish as she's acting, she's a big girl (and you can't send her to her room—much as you would like to). Sooner or later, she's going to catch a breeze from the cold shoulder everyone is giving her—and that's when she'll snap out of it.

Ⓔ ESSENTIAL

Be very specific with your complaints. *Don't* say, "You're just being so nasty, I can't believe it!" Give her very specific examples, and present them in a calm voice: "When you commented on the caterer's weight problem, it was very rude and incredibly insensitive, *and* it embarrassed me."

She's All Right . . . Really

The bride who holds it together throughout the entire planning process is a rare bird, but she's not extinct. Brides who lean toward simple affairs often do so for the benefit of their own mental health. This is not to say that a bride who is planning an elaborate ceremony and reception is automatically headed for a breakdown. Some women really are able to handle a wedding in the midst of an already busy life.

Be on the lookout for the bride who keeps her cool until she slips into her wedding gown—and all of the planning and preparations suddenly translate into reality (so *that's* why she was so calm . . .). You can help this bride out by assuring her that everything is going to be fine, and that she's well prepared for this day and for the future. Prepare *yourself* to be on high alert throughout the course of the day to ward off a potential bridal meltdown.

 **ALERT!**

If your daughter is holding herself together better than you expected, consider yourself fortunate. Just be careful that you don't drive her over the edge by unwittingly expecting too much of her *because* she's doing so well. She *does* need help, even if she isn't asking for it.

The Groom's Family

Many times, two families will come together and realize that they're all rational people, and everyone will make an effort to get along with one another. Pleasant relationships ensue. However, once in a while, a young man and a young woman from two incredibly different sets of parents will decide to get married, which forces their respective parents together—at least temporarily. How can you facilitate the transition from being strangers (strangers who, by the way, would never speak to each other under normal circumstances) to being amicable coplanners of this wedding?

Meeting of the Minds

Even when you're trying to be open-minded and accepting of others, your relationship with the groom's parents might still be strained. If you're experiencing great difficulty working side by side with these folks, should you just throw in the towel? Avoid them? Have it out with them?

There's *always* hope for a peaceful resolution to personality conflicts. If world leaders from different cultures can come together and work out *their* differences, surely you can hammer out an understanding or two with these folks. How, you ask? Keep this little checklist in mind:

❑ **Be honest with yourself.** If you find the groom's parents are not to your liking, is it because they're truly offensive? Is it possible that you're reacting to traits that are simply *different* from your own personality?

❑ **Don't judge.** If the groom's father has been divorced three times, don't write him off as a womanizer. If his mom never smiles, don't assume she hates you. These are traits that really don't affect *your* life, and you probably don't have all the facts, anyway. Don't make them into big issues.

❑ **Communicate openly.** It's hard for some people to say what's on their mind. When you're planning a wedding, though, it's important for everyone to know what everyone else is thinking. Plans have to be made; bills have to be paid. Speak up!

You might not end up being especially close with the groom's parents, and that's all right. It's not wise to try to force a friendship. You want to avoid any misunderstandings, however—misunderstandings at this point in your relationship could undermine any good vibes you've got going with them. You're working with a clean slate; fill it up with facts—not assumptions.

Speaking of Speaking Up . . .

It's important to acknowledge any differences and work through them, rather than simply trying to block them out. Contrary to popular belief, ignoring problems doesn't make them go away—in fact, ignoring a difficult situation with your daughter's future in-laws might just escalate the problem to the point where it's impossible to deal with it without seriously offending someone.

Take, for example, an MOG who is not your idea of a perfect cohost. She's trying to run the show, even though you're paying for most of it; maybe she's even butting in on your territory (choosing her dress first and telling *you* what color to wear). What tack do you take with her?

Ignoring her would seem like a good option—except she won't *be* ignored. A busybody like this will keep nosing her way in, because she truly feels as though her way is the *only* right way to do things. She may be a very nice woman otherwise, which makes dealing with her even more difficult since you don't want to offend her; you just want to get on with planning the wedding—*without* her.

It's best to be forthcoming in your communications with the in-laws, and the sooner the better, because eventually everything will be out in the open. If you wait until this woman has driven you absolutely insane with her incessant phone calls and her attempts to "help" you (by booking a banquet hall you didn't ask her to reserve—one you never would have chosen, for example), you're going to be far less diplomatic when you finally tell her that you don't need her assistance.

ⓔ ESSENTIAL

> Don't offend the groom's family by completely shutting them out of the wedding. Alienating these people so that you can control every aspect of the planning is just a bad idea. It's a big day for them, too. Let them in on the preparations if they want to help.

The New Man in the Family

Once the planning of the wedding begins, you'll find out what sort of son-in-law you're *really* getting. Oh sure, when they got engaged, you had a nice, long talk with your daughter's fiancé—but you can probably assume correctly that he was on his very best behavior at that point. When the planning kicks into full swing, his real personality will come out. Is he really as sweet as you thought, or is he trying to crash your party planning? Is it all right for you to get along very, very well with him?

And how do you handle a groom who's wearing on your nerves?

He Really *Is* Perfect

Congratulations! Your daughter has chosen a laid-back, fairly successful, humorous young man who is also kind to animals and senior citizens. He doesn't have a flaw that you can think of, and he's been even more help to you during the wedding planning than your daughter has. You're happy, he's happy, the bride's happy . . .

Except she doesn't seem happy. In fact, she's been short with you and her fiancé, and she definitely seems bugged by your relationship with him. What could possibly be the problem, you ask. It couldn't be that she's feeling left out—she's your daughter; she's your baby; she knows how much you love her. In fact, part of the reason you've been so accepting of the groom is because you want your daughter to be happy. No one wants an MOB and a groom to be at odds with each other.

Keep in mind that brides are often not in top emotional form during their engagements. She sees you and the groom getting along swell; meanwhile, you and *she* have been at each other's throats over some of the planning issues. She could perceive this as a certain type of favoritism on your part. The groom will also be suspect in her mind—why is he cozying up to *you*? (He has his *own* mother!) While you want the best possible relationship with your future son-in-law, just be careful that the two of you aren't getting too close for the bride's comfort—or she might make darn sure that *no one* is happy.

Ⓔ ALERT!

> Believe it or not, the bride could object to you and the groom getting along too well with one another. Make sure that in your haste to accept the groom as a perfect male specimen that you aren't making your daughter feel like an outsider.

Who's In Charge Here, Anyway?

How can it be that this man your daughter is going to marry—the one who is grating on your nerves—is the same guy you liked so much when they first announced their engagement? He was much nicer back then—or at least you *think* he was. His specific traits aren't important— perhaps he's started to show a bit of a bossy side since the topics of the ceremony and reception have been introduced; maybe he's kind of arrogant, assuming his ideas are better than yours; perhaps he simply talks too much about what he envisions as the perfect wedding day. Whatever the case, you're trying to plan a big reception here, and he keeps getting in your way somehow. Quite frankly, you're about to throw in the towel and tell him to plan the darn thing himself. Don't be so quick to threaten—he might just take you up on the offer.

Problems can arise when the groom has specific ideas for his wedding that don't gel with your own thoughts. The troubles can multiply when you're paying for everything, and he's trying to dictate the plans. What are you supposed to do? Tell him to butt out of his own wedding? Hand him your checkbook and let him go wild? The answer lies somewhere in the middle. You'll have to discuss which aspects of the wedding are most important to each of you, and go from there.

 FACT

> Although traditionally the MOB handles the wedding planning, nowadays that task is seemingly up for grabs. While not all MOBs will want to oversee the wedding, many will . . . and will find themselves competing with any number of other interested parties for the chore.

Of course, if you're shelling out for the entire thing, you'll have much more of an influence on the final decisions—but it doesn't mean that you can automatically veto the groom's wishes. You want him to feel comfortable at his wedding, don't you? And you don't want this wedding to be a sore subject between the two of you for the rest of your lives, as it could be if one of you snatches the wedding baton and runs solo with it. Find a way to *compromise* with him, and you'll make things easier on yourself in the long run.

Keeping the Guests Informed

Chances are, unless you and the bride are surrounded by your entire family and all of your friends on a daily basis, you're going to end up inviting *someone* from outside of your immediate area. (And even if *your* entire side of the guest list resides within a mile of the ceremony and reception sites, the groom's whole family may be coming from across the country to attend the wedding.) Sending your guests timely invitations is, of course, your first concern when it comes to keeping them informed. But there *are* ways to go beyond the call of duty, to really make them feel as though you truly are grateful for their presence, and to show that you're bound and determined to look out for your guests.

Save-the-Date Cards

These preinvitation mailings are becoming more popular with brides and grooms. As free time seems to be a lost commodity for everyone in this day and age, couples who are headed to the altar want to make sure that their guests have adequate time to clear their schedules and make travel arrangements for the wedding.

Is the save-the-date card your problem? Not really, but the bride may ask for your opinion and/or advice—in which case, you'll need to know what kind of information the cards should include and when they should be sent out. For starters, these cards can be very formal or very *in*formal. (They can even be handmade, if the couple—or at least half of the couple—is artistically inclined.) The information included on the card is very basic: the names of your daughter and her fiancé, the date of the wedding, and the words "Save the date." You may also want to include, "Invitation to follow." Though the couple can mail the cards out as soon as they have chosen a wedding date, sending them out several months before the wedding is also perfectly acceptable.

 ALERT!

Brides and grooms who are planning a ceremony during the hectic summer months will not only be competing with *other* engaged couples for their guests' presence, but also with treasured vacation times. Here's where save-the-date cards can mean the difference between a church filled with guests . . . and an empty sanctuary.

Obviously, these cards are only sent to people who will be included on the guest list. If your family and the groom's family are all living in the same town, these cards are probably not necessary, especially if the wedding and reception are going to be held locally. However, if your guest list includes scores of out-of-town guests, they may really appreciate having advance notice of the wedding, as they may have to juggle their schedules around and start watching for cheap plane fares in order to attend.

Tour Guide MOB

You've got guests coming from all over the country, and none of them are familiar with your hometown. You don't want to end up with a house filled with guests, and you also don't want to be fielding calls from guests who can't seem to find the church and who have no idea where they can grab a quick bite to eat.

Reserve a block of rooms at a local hotel for out-of-town guests. Scope the place out yourself first and make sure it's clean enough for the guests who will expect decent accommodations. Also try to choose a place that's within the average guest's means. (Melding these two qualities under one roof isn't all that difficult; however, if you have a feeling that Aunt Betty will object to sleeping in a three-star place, you might want to have the number of the five-star hotel handy.) Include the hotel's name and telephone number on the invitations, along with any special instructions (such as, "Guests of the Smith wedding will be given a special rate if rooms are reserved by May eighth").

Make things *really* easy on everyone by including a map of the area with the invitations, along with explicit, handwritten directions from the hotel to the church, and from the church to the reception site. Unfortunately, not everyone can follow instructions to travel *west* or *south* on a bustling boulevard. Your sense-of-direction-impaired guests will appreciate knowing whether they should turn *right* or *left*, and will probably kiss you if you include landmarks along the way, so that they know for certain they're headed in the right direction.

Chapter 7
Delicate Situations

You were doing just fine, living in your own little world—and then your daughter decided to have a big wedding. This, of course, means you'll be forced to reckon with the past—or perhaps a less-than-pleasant set of current circumstances. Former husbands, relatives you thought (or maybe hoped) were long gone, and step-relations will be popping up all over the place, like dandelions in the spring. You'll be happy to see some of them, no doubt . . . but what do you do with the others?

Bye-Bye, Love

If you split with your husband eons ago, by now the two of you may have worked out a peaceful (if distant) coexistence. The kids haven't heard the two of you argue with each other in a decade or more, and your lives are completely separate at this point. Even if you aren't exactly the best of friends, this is a somewhat amicable relationship. The two of you really are better off apart, and your children are happier for it, too. If this describes you, the wedding plans will most likely proceed without a lot of infighting and backbiting. (Whew!)

If, on the other hand, the divorce was more recent (say, *very* recent), and there are still unresolved issues between you and the man who used to be your spouse, this wedding could be the thing that takes your relationship from bad to worse. Why? A daughter's wedding is an emotional experience for people who are feeling fairly *stable* in their lives—it goes without saying that it can be doubly (or triply) so for parents of the bride who are at odds with one another.

Mr. Moneybags

Money is a huge flash point in many divorces. If your husband owes you a bundle from the sale of joint property, for example, and he's been dragging his feet on cutting you a check, you may have very mixed emotions when he sweeps into town offering to pay for your daughter's entire wedding. He's her hero right now, regardless of their prior relationship. Sure, you're happy that she's going to get the wedding she's always dreamed of, but you're scraping by every month. You can't afford to contribute much at this point, which makes you feel awful—but if your ex would just hand over the money you're owed, you could come off looking like super parent, too.

 ALERT!

> The last thing you want to do is to get your child tangled up in the financial mess that often follows a divorce. You especially wouldn't want to make the bride feel as though you begrudge her the money her father is so generously offering.

What do you do when your ex isn't playing fair with the wedding finances? Sit back and watch as money that is rightfully yours is spent on flowers and bonbons—while you rack up more and more in life-related debt? Your best bet is to shut down any chance of this happening in the first place. When your daughter first becomes engaged, let your ex know that you won't allow him to throw money at her until he's given you what's yours. This is not a matter of pettiness, as you well know—it's a matter of fairness and a matter of necessity, as well. Chances are, one way or the other, your daughter is going to have a splendid wedding. It would be nice, though, if you and her dad could *both* be benefactors of the big day.

The New Mrs.

Your husband has a new wife in his life, and she seems to have definite ideas for your daughter's wedding. Unless you and your ex's wife are friendly with one another (which is not an uncommon situation—though you should still consider yourself lucky if the two of you can be civil to each other), you might find yourself preparing to go head-to-head with her over the menu, the reception site, and the guest list. This is not how you envisioned your role as MOB—you thought you would be the *only* MOB.

Ⓔ **ESSENTIAL**

If you're sharing the MOB duties with your daughter's stepmother, be as courteous and as civil as possible (you want to be *dual* MOBs, not *dueling* MOBs). Your daughter should make the final decisions as to which duties you and her stepmom will have.

First off, you have to take stock of what's really going on between you and your ex's new wife. If the two of you have a longstanding feud with one another, trying to coplan a wedding is going to be difficult at best. Because weddings are such an emotional time, there's a chance that you'll be more irritated than usual with each other as you try to compromise without *really* giving into her (or her to you) on anything. On the other hand, this could be a perfect time for you two to finally realize what's important (apparently, your daughter is important enough to both of you that you want to make sure the wedding is beautiful) and what isn't (namely, the past).

Another thing to consider is how much each of you is throwing into the wedding jackpot. While it may not seem fair to you, if your ex-husband is paying for most of this wedding, his wife *does* have a right to pipe up now and then regarding the details. If the bride has a real problem with her stepmother's opinions, that's a whole separate issue, and the way to handle it is unique to each family. Your daughter might feel comfortable putting her foot down on certain issues, or she may appeal to her father—or she just might come to you to intervene on her behalf.

Unless you and the stepmother are on good terms, this is a risky proposition. Nothing good will come of your middleman approach; in fact, it will probably make things much worse all the way around, for many reasons:

- Your ex's wife will feel (and rightly so, most likely) that you and your daughter are teaming up against her.
- Your ex will be forced to actively choose a side. Family turmoil will follow.
- These are the types of fights that go on *forever*, precisely because the atmosphere surrounding a wedding is so emotional.

Implore your daughter to act like an adult and to be assertive with her stepmother, or to appeal to her dad.

The Bride's Stepdad

Your husband is a man among men. He happens to be the bride's stepfather, and she also happens to be very close to her "real dad." You fear that someone's feelings are going to be hurt along the way, because, after all, only one of these men can escort her down the aisle. How can you persuade her to choose your husband, who is, after all, the dad who's physically been around all of these years?

 FACT

> If the bride's father is deceased, she may choose to have one of her brothers escort her down the aisle, even if you remarried years and years ago. A stepfather should walk her down the aisle only if it's her choice, and only if they're close.

You can't. This is completely the bride's choice, and no matter what's happened between you and her dad (or her and her dad) over the years, she shouldn't be pressured or guilted into choosing one man over the other. Even if you think she's making a wrong choice and basing it on sentimentality, zip the lip. It's her wedding, and this is what she wants. This is one thing that is absolutely not up to you to criticize or attempt to influence.

Now, as for how your former and current hubbies are going to deal with one another . . . men are usually pretty good about staying out of each other's way when they don't care for one another. Yes, it's completely sexist and politically incorrect to say so, but women are more likely to get catty with their sworn enemies, and are also more likely to recruit other women into joining the fray. Unless men have huge issues to work out (one has stolen money from the other, or one has stolen a wife from the other), they're content to leave each other alone and get on with life. If your husband and your ex have very little to do with each other, and barely acknowledge each other's existence, you can't expect them to act chummy at the reception; just be thankful they're not roping off the dance floor for a fight to the finish.

An Ex-Family Reunion

Of course, when a man becomes your ex, his relatives become your former in-laws. Depending on the circumstances, they may also have formerly liked you. Do you really have to extend the guest list to these people who constantly badmouth you, who will no doubt make you feel uncomfortable, and who will only serve to dredge up images of days gone by that you would rather forget?

If this were your wedding, you could completely discard these folks and surround yourself with people who would only heap praise and compliments on you for the entire day. Of course, this *isn't* your party, technically speaking, no matter how much money and energy you've put into it. Your former relations are your daughter's blood relatives, and as long as *she's* not actively doing battle with them, you have to respect that bond. You can't exclude your former mother-in-law, whom you like to refer to as "evil woman," because as far as your daughter is concerned, she's Grandma. What's happened between the two of you must be put aside for one day.

Ⓔ ESSENTIAL

Try as you might, you can't completely prevent the possibility of unpleasant exchanges between warring former family factions. But you can make things infinitely easier on yourself simply by maintaining a healthy amount of space from anyone who's likely to start trouble with you.

You'll be incredibly busy on the day of the wedding, looking out for your daughter, making sure that everything's going according to plan, and you won't have time to worry about what your former brother-in-law might be saying about you at any given moment. Unfortunately, some folks go out of their way to start trouble by initiating face-to-face confrontations. Any fool knows that a wedding is one of the least appropriate places to revisit old arguments. Your best bet is to simply ignore anyone who tries to pull you into a fight. If the behavior is really out of bounds (shouting, cursing, etc.), you have every right to ask a troublemaker to leave. Your daughter and her groom (and his entire family) shouldn't have to bear witness to such ugliness on their big day.

Step Right Up

When your stepdaughter gets engaged, what's your official title? Are you the SMOB (stepmother of the bride)? Are you responsible for *anything*, as far as this wedding is concerned, or does most of the work fall squarely on the shoulders of your husband's former wife? As weddings veer further and further off the traditional track, you'll find that every situation involving a stepmother and a bride-to-be is unique.

Your involvement in the wedding will depend on your stepdaughter's relationship with her dad, her relationship with her mother, and her relationship with you. Proceed with the utmost caution, and no one will be able to criticize your moves.

Stepmom Straits

Your stepdaughter has come home wearing an engagement ring. Your husband is planning on paying for most of the wedding. Where do you fit in *now*? Some concerns a stepmother of the bride may have include:

- **Your duties.** Are you the hostess, or simply the wife of the host?
- **The finances.** Is the bride's mom the official sponsor of the reception, although the checks have been written out of your joint account?
- **The invitations.** Can you invite your family, or is that tacky?

When the split has been amicable and both of the bride's parents are involved in the wedding, most brides will send out an invitation that includes the names of both sets of parents, indicating cosponsorship. As far as inviting your family is concerned, you'll want to consider whether they have anything to do with your stepdaughter. If your brother barely knows the bride, for example, she may wonder why he's being included in the celebration of her marriage.

Are You In or Out?

Will you be called on to help with the planning? You might be, especially if you have some interesting connections in town (say, your best friend is a florist, or you happen to know a world-class violinist who just *might* be talked into soloing at the ceremony)—but you might not be. If you're very, very close to your stepdaughter, she'll probably be sensitive enough to realize that excluding you from the planning could be very hurtful to you. If the two of you get along pretty well but aren't exactly soul mates, she may simply lean on her mom.

(E) ALERT!

Remember that the bride is going through this process for the first time. She might forget about you altogether—not because she wants to insult you, but simply because it hasn't occurred to her to include you. Don't take it personally, especially if your relationship up to this point has been ideal.

The Wedding Day

If your stepdaughter chose to live with her dad after the divorce, you and your husband will occupy the best seats in church, in the front row; if she stayed with her mom, the two of you will be seated in the third row. At the reception, you may not be required to stand in the receiving line. Regardless, get inside, greet the guests as they enter the area set up with cocktails and appetizers, and be a gracious cohostess. Touch base with the bride's mom now and then to see if you can lend a hand somewhere, but don't steal her limelight. (That advice goes double for your dress—choose something that complements the bride's mother's gown, but that doesn't completely upstage her.)

Keeping the Peace

As if working out the roles for moms and stepmoms and dads and stepdads wasn't difficult enough, it's suddenly occurred to you that all of you will be under one roof at the ceremony and reception—and possibly at several parties before the wedding. To top it all off, the groom's parents are also divorced, and their situation is not what anyone would call friendly.

Is it in everyone's best interest to simply keep the pre-wedding parties separate, and to graciously exclude one parent from each family from the reception? That would make life so much easier, but it's really not appropriate to decide that one parent has to miss their child's wedding. All of the parents concerned are adults, and should be held to adult standards of conduct.

ⓔ ESSENTIAL

Your daughter has already lived through your divorce once. Don't reopen old wounds by exchanging nastiness with your ex now. Regardless of your own experience, do your best to make sure that your daughter enters into marriage thinking it's a *good* thing.

Pre-Wedding Parties

If there's a horrific split in the family (between you and the bride's father, or between the groom's parents), it's best to keep the guest list for any pre-wedding parties as small and as simple as possible. If you're hosting a small engagement party, for example, you don't need to invite your ex and his new wife and their entire extended families. The bride's father always has the option of hosting a separate engagement celebration.

Showers should also be handled tactfully. If your divorce set off a series of rumblings in your ex's family (and the result is that you are not welcome in their homes, and they are not welcome in yours), there's no sense in trying to force everyone together for an afternoon of forced niceties (or worse, an afternoon of sparring). Since showers are really not required to have a bridesmaid as hostess in this day and age, your ex's family is more than welcome to host their own shower for the bride.

In Church

Keeping everyone apart for the duration of the engagement is one thing: There can be multiple, separate parties for the bride and groom during which former family members need never cross paths. Not so with the wedding—the bride usually only gets one ceremony, and it's up to her (and you) to figure out a way to keep the peace over the course of the day.

In the case of a nasty divorce, the FOB may still escort his daughter down the aisle (much to her mother's chagrin), but he will most likely be seated in the third row, while the MOB and her hubby (if she has remarried) are seated in the first row. If your daughter chose to live with her dad after the divorce, she may flip-flop these seating arrangements so that he has the front-row view of the ceremony (along with the bride's stepmother, if there's a new wife on the scene). Roll with this if it happens; it's an approved law of etiquette—*not* a move which is designed to hurt or humiliate you.

Ⓔ ESSENTIAL

The first row is a place of honor for the parent who has actually raised the bride; this may or may not be the same person who is paying for the wedding. You could theoretically end up paying for most of the ceremony and still find yourself without a front-row seat.

Imagine yourself as the bride. Imagine your own parents embroiled in a nasty, ongoing feud that has yet to show any signs of weakening. Now imagine you're standing at that altar, ready to take your own vows, and all you can think about is whether your mom or dad is going to say something horrible to the other one at any moment. This is the entire reason for the first row/third row separation of combative parents.

At the Reception

With all the milling around that goes on during receptions, an ex is bound to cross paths with his or her former better half. The new wife and the former wife will eventually run into one another in the ladies' room. The former husband and the current husband will bump elbows at the bar. Are there rules for how these people should interact?

In fact, there are. The rules are called *common sense*. No matter how much your ex-husband gets under your skin, your daughter's wedding is neither the time nor the place to correct his flaws. If his new wife is shimmying shamelessly all over the dance floor, just remember that her actions don't reflect on *you*, and it's really not up to you to stop her squirming.

Ⓔ **ALERT!**

Get creative with the seating arrangements *without getting nasty*. Seat the bride's father as close to the head table as possible, so that he's still in a place of honor, but there's at least one group between your table and his. Seating him near the broom closet is just not nice.

While the dance floor, the bar, and the powder room are areas beyond your control, you can make sure that dinner is a pleasant experience for everyone by giving fractured families lots of room to relax. If you've had a particularly bitter split with the bride's father, for example, you may literally feel sick when you look at him. Make sure you won't have to—and especially not while you're eating. Seat your ex and his family several tables away from you.

Special Roles

Godparents and grandparents are often recognized as VIPs during a wedding ceremony. Grandparents should be seated toward the front of the church, and the groom's grandparents are shown to their seats before the bride's grandma and grandpa. The bride and groom often order boutonnieres for the grandfathers and corsages for the grandmothers. Grandparents are seated near the head table at the reception, often with the parents of the bride or groom.

If your daughter has kept a close relationship with her godparents, she may want to ask them to bring up the gifts in church, or to do a reading, or to hand out programs before the ceremony. She may also order a corsage for her godmother or a boutonniere for her godfather. If she hasn't seen these people since she was baptized, however, and they haven't made any special effort to keep her on the straight and narrow by teaching her about her religion, they don't require any special recognition (or even an invitation, for that matter).

Second Weddings

You thought your daughter's first time down the aisle would also be her last, but you were wrong. As if educating yourself on how to run the first wedding wasn't enough, now you're faced with a second wedding, and you have no idea how to handle the particulars. Should the bride have another huge wedding if she wants one? Is it really inappropriate for her to walk down the aisle, to have her dad give her away, for her to wear white?

The Size and Shape of Things

Traditional etiquette states that a second wedding ceremony should be an intimate affair, whether the bride or groom has been widowed or divorced. Where death has ended a union, a small second ceremony shows respect for the dearly departed; when the bride or groom has been divorced, etiquette mavens encourage a quiet second wedding to discourage less-than-kind onlookers from pointing out that one of the interested parties has already broken the very vows that he or she is reciting again.

Ⓔ ESSENTIAL

While the second ceremony is sometimes a small affair, the reception can include as many guests as the bride and groom want, and can be as lavish as they can afford to make it. In the case of a second wedding, guests are fairly understanding about only being invited to the reception.

Now here's a bit of news: There are no etiquette cops (or at least none that are armed). If your daughter wants another big wedding this time around, chances are, her decision will be based on more practical manners (such as money and how many guests she wants to invite) than on the ins and outs of social graces. This is another example of tradition going out the window—for better or for worse (you may not be sure which yet).

Ⓔ **QUESTION**

Can a bride wear white to her second wedding?
Traditional etiquette would say no; white is a symbol of purity and is supposed to signify a virgin bride. However, second-time brides are not held to this rigid rule nowadays. Trains *are* frowned upon at the second wedding, though; suits or floor-length gowns are popular choices.

If the bride has chosen to have a quiet ceremony, she may have only one or two attendants. The bride herself may choose to wear a simple gown or a bridal suit instead of a wedding gown. What will *you* wear, then? Follow the bride's lead. If she's chosen something knee length and fairly understated, your dress should be even more understated. (In other words, don't try to sneak into the ceremony wearing a floor-length beaded gown while the bride is dressed in a tea-length, off-the-rack dress. *Someone* is going to notice that you're more done-up than your daughter is.)

Who's Got the Check?

The bride and groom usually pay for a second wedding, and list themselves as hosts on the invitations. If you and your husband would like to contribute to the wedding or reception, no one will stop you; however, if your daughter had a big old wedding the first time around and you have no intention of handing over one cent for this event, hardly anyone will fault you for that decision (except, perhaps, your daughter).

Don't make the money issue a personal matter between you and the bride. If you thought she made a huge mistake in either marrying or divorcing her first husband, the worst thing you could do right now is to tell her, "I will *not* pay for your second wedding, because you should have stayed married to Bill in the first place!" (Oooh . . . *harsh,* Mom.) She's in a certain position in life; she can't go back in time and change the events that brought her to this point. You don't have to pay for a second wedding, but *don't* call her judgment into question now.

The Kids

If your daughter has children, should they be at the second wedding? You want to shield your grandkids from any discomfort, and if the little ones (or not-so-little ones) aren't exactly thrilled about the prospect of acquiring a stepfather, shouldn't they just stay home instead—or go to a movie?

 FACT

> Many brides and grooms include their children in a second wedding ceremony. In addition to making the kids feel important for an afternoon, encouraging the feeling that they're all in this together can go a long way towards easing the transition into being an actual family.

Even if your daughter's children aren't happy about their mom's wedding, they should absolutely be there. Her marriage vows *will* take them into a new reality, whether they like it or not, and there isn't a worse way to start off that new life than by boycotting this event. Do everything in your power to convince older kids that they should be at the ceremony and reception—because if they're allowed to skip it, everyone is instantly put into an awkward position: Your daughter's husband will feel insulted and/or angry, the kids will instantly be at odds with their new stepfather, and your daughter will be in the middle. There will be lots and lots of time to work out the big issues after the wedding. For now, everyone needs to show support for one another—even if it hurts a little.

Chapter 8
Doing the Legwork

It takes certain inquisitive skills to plan a wedding. There's good news and bad news here: The good news is that the wedding industry on the whole is huge, and you'll most likely be able to find just about every service you're looking for. The bad news (which isn't really all *that* bad, actually) is that it's going to take a lot of effort from whoever is leading the planning brigade. Get some rest, and then start pounding the pavement.

Preparing Yourself for the Interviews

You may feel as though you're going to get an education when you sit down to discuss the particulars of this wedding with certain vendors. That's not the case. You should go out of your way to educate yourself *before* you meet face-to-face with a banquet manager or a baker or a florist. You don't want to be hit with sticker shock while you're interviewing the photographer, and you definitely don't want to end up paying too much for anything. (Even if money isn't a particular worry of yours, why pay Photographer A 25 percent more than Photographer B for the same exact services?)

Pass It On!

One of the best ways to get a line on who's reputable and who isn't (and which vendors offer the best services) is through word of mouth. You can start asking around as soon as your daughter has some idea of what type of wedding she's leaning toward. Don't worry if you don't have any close friends or family members who have recently gone through the wedding process. Anyone who has been to a wedding recently is a good enough resource: She can tell you if the food was good, if the band was off-key, and whether the photographer took lots of pictures of the guests. If your curiosity is piqued (in a *good* way), she can give you the name of the bride, who will most likely be happy to share her insight with you, even if you're a perfect stranger. (Many brides are extremely accommodating when it comes to helping engaged women or MOBs in this manner.)

Ⓔ FACT

You'll want to get a good idea of what things should cost before you start making appointments with various vendors. For example, you probably won't be able to find a photographer who offers a $100 wedding package—and if you do, you probably shouldn't hire him.

Other research tools include wedding magazines and books, and the Internet. These are especially helpful for finding the latest trends in weddings. (If your daughter just has to have wild exotic flowers at her reception, you can bring a picture from a magazine with you when you meet with the florist, and she can tell you whether she's capable of reproducing such glory.) Remember to organize your information and to take a notebook along with you. You'll have a lot of information thrown at you. In order to make the best decision, you'll have to sort through prices and services at some point, which is going to be difficult to do if you're relying solely on your memory, or if you can't find the price lists.

Learn by Example

One last way to do your research is to start making the reception rounds. This will give you a good idea of how a band really sounds or how a reception hall really handles several hundred guests. Most banquet managers and bandleaders (and other vendors, as well) will give you dates and times so that you can see their work in progress. Even if you're 99.9 percent sure that you want the Twist and Shouts to perform at your daughter's reception, it's best to see them in action first.

Don't worry about looking or feeling out of place if you don't know a soul—chances are, some of the invited guests feel as awkward as you do. Besides, no one ever needs to know who you are (or *aren't*, in this case).

What Are You Getting Yourself Into?

Once you've met with the vendors, you'll narrow your choices down, and at some point, you'll want to wheel and deal with them. Be aware that you're really not in a position to wheel *or* deal, because most reputable vendors (especially in the busy wedding months, from April to October) have all the business they need. They don't need to give you a break, because there's usually someone else in line right behind you who's willing to pay full price.

The most popular wedding and reception sites are often booked solid a year and a half to two years in advance, so you may well feel as though you're under the gun even if you've gotten an early start in your planning. Don't let pressure blind you. Take a good look at what you're being offered by various vendors, and what you're going to end up paying for—and don't sign a contract until you're completely comfortable with the terms of it.

ESSENTIAL

If you're planning an extraordinarily large wedding, you might be able to negotiate a lower price per head with a banquet hall, due to the sheer volume of business you're offering. In the slower winter wedding season, some vendors offer lower prices, as well.

Read the fine print. You just might find something there that will keep you awake nights. For example, if your daughter has her heart set on using a certain photographer, but he's not willing to work with the wedding day schedule—he wants to show up at noon to take pictures of the entire wedding party when the wedding isn't until five o'clock—he's not the best guy for the job. (He's probably trying to squeeze a game of golf into his Saturday.) His attempt to put his job (the one *you're* paying him for, by the way) way down on his list of priorities speaks volumes about what you can expect from this joker. Look elsewhere for someone who will give your daughter's wedding day photos the attention they deserve.

The Ceremony

The ceremony can take place just about anywhere there's room for people to gather (and *that* depends, of course, on whether the bride and groom are looking to have a small, intimate exchange of vows or a ceremony that the entire town can attend). Many brides still opt for the traditional church wedding, though others look for a more unique site. Either way, booking the ceremony site isn't always as easy as making one phone call (though you'd think it should be).

A Good Old Church Wedding

Depending on the church the bride and groom have chosen, they may be able to waltz right down the aisle, or they may have a few hoops to jump through. More and more churches are encouraging (or requiring) premarital classes for engaged couples. Catholic churches often impose a waiting period of at least six months for brides and grooms (which means if the bride calls the office in November to schedule her ceremony, she won't be able to say "I do" until May). Smaller churches with fewer members may be able to squeeze a ceremony in on relatively short notice.

The bride and groom need to be prepared with a list of questions during their initial interview with their officiant. They'll want to know, for example, about the specific requirements for marriage in this particular church; the cost of using the building for the ceremony (usually referred to as a "donation"); whether the time and date they're hoping for is available; any restrictions on music, pictures or videos, or decorations; whether another wedding is scheduled to immediately follow theirs (if so, can the parking lot handle the traffic?); and any other requirements or restrictions.

 FACT

Even if both the bride and groom have grown up in a particular church and their parents are members, some churches also require that the bride and groom become registered members before they can be married there.

Civil Sites for the Ceremony

The official reasoning behind many of the stringent church requirements for marriage is to encourage engaged couples to move toward adulthood and take stock of what marriage is really about (which, in light of the divorce rate these days, is hardly objectionable). However, many brides and grooms rebel against being forced into compliance, and *really* object to being forced into joining a church that they've always attended (a move seen by some engaged couples as a grab for more money). These are some of the reasons civil ceremonies are gaining in popularity among men and women who would otherwise take a more traditional wedding route.

The words "civil ceremony" sometimes promote an image of city hall—but the truth is, a civil ceremony can be as formal as a cathedral wedding. If the bride is hankering to get married outside of the confines of her church or temple, all the two of you need is a bit of creativity. The possibilities are really endless, and are basically dependent on where the bride and groom would be most comfortable on their wedding day.

 FACT

> Some clergy members will perform a religious ceremony in a civil location; some will also perform ceremonies with clergy of a different religion during an interfaith ceremony. Catholic priests will insist on a Catholic wedding in a Catholic church.

For a nonchurch wedding, consider:

- A yacht club or marina
- A garden in the park or botanical preserve
- An upscale restaurant
- An art gallery or museum
- Historic homes or inns
- Old royal theaters

The upside to having a wedding at a civil spot is that the reception is *right there*; no one has to scramble to make it to the hall after the ceremony, and there's also no delay. The bride and groom get hitched and everyone eats. The downside is that it can be a lot of work to coordinate the site, the officiant, and the caterer—you're dealing with three schedules as opposed to two (with a church wedding and a banquet hall with on-site chefs). It can also be more expensive to hire a caterer than to work with a reception facility that provides these services.

The Food

No matter where the ceremony is going to take place, you're going to have to feed the guests at some point, and you're going to want to feed them well. Food is one of the things that can make or break the wedding day. Many guests won't notice the decorations, some will ignore the beauty of the ceremony altogether, and no one except the bride and groom will get to enjoy the pictures. The quality and quantity of the food will make some sort of impression on every single guest, and while it's true that you'll never be able to please everyone, a horrible reception dinner is sure to *disappoint* everyone. (And you will still have spent a bundle on the inedible meal.) Might as well make it worth your money and go for the good stuff.

Banquet Hall Considerations

If the reception is scheduled to take place at a relatively upscale reception facility—a banquet hall, a hotel ballroom, a restaurant—you'll most likely end up working with their on-site staff. Some of these places will let you bring in your own caterer; many won't, simply because they're already set up for the entire operation, and if you bring in your own people, they're losing money on the deal.

ESSENTIAL

Be sure to request a taste test. You're going to be shelling out quite a bit for some good eats; you shouldn't be expected to choose the menu without knowing what's to your liking and what isn't.

Meeting with the banquet manager should be a fairly pleasant experience. It's this person's job to inform you about the site and the services offered there. Most places have a fairly wide variety of packages, ranging from cocktail receptions to seven-course dinners and beyond, so you should be able to find what you're looking for. (If you don't, look somewhere *else*.) The manager will give you a tour of the facility, making sure to highlight certain areas (the terrace, which is perfect for pictures, or the lush and private bride's room), hoping to grab your attention (and your business). What will probably be most important to you and the bride is whether a certain site can meet your needs, whether they can come close to your price, and, simply, whether you like it or not.

Some things to ask about the location:

- How many guests can they handle comfortably?
- Is the dinner a sit-down affair? Buffet? Stations?
- Where will the band set up? Where is the dance floor?
- How will the staff dress? How many servers will there be?
- Will your head count have to include band members and the photographer?
- Can the site provide a cake, or will you have to find a baker? Is there a cake-cutting fee?
- Is there an extra fee for a champagne toast?
- What is the cost of an open bar? How many hours does the price include?
- Is there an extra charge for valet parking or a coatroom attendant?
- How much of a deposit is required? When is the full balance due?
- Are there any other fees?

If you don't like what you're hearing, but you love the actual surroundings, close your eyes and think. It's not worth the money you'll spend if the place is short-staffed, your guests will be squeezed into their seats, and it costs extra for nice table linens (the dingy brown tablecloths are available at no extra cost). The reception is usually the most expensive part of a wedding; make sure you're getting what you want from the deal.

Finding a Caterer

If the bride and groom decide to take their wedding on the road, you'll have to find someone to follow—with chafing dishes and food. Finding a good caterer isn't all that difficult. Many restaurants offer catering service, for one thing, and you've probably had catered food without even realizing it (at business meetings or other functions). Ask around if you're clueless; someone you know will be able to point you in the right direction.

 FACT

Good food isn't *that* hard to find. If you haven't found a caterer yet, start hitting the wedding shows. Caterers flock to these events and will be able to answer your questions and send you home with some literature.

When you've found someone who specializes in the type of event you're planning (be it formal or informal), you'll have a few inquiries. You'll want to know, for example, how long they've been in business, what size events they normally handle, and whether they can provide you with references from other weddings they've done. You'll want to make sure they have any permits that are required by law (it would be a shame if they were shut down by the Health Department a week before your daughter's big day) and whether they're insured. You'll ask about deposits and final payments, as well as the cost of the bar and when the final head count is due.

Other questions you'll want to ask:

- What are your options? Can you have stations, sit-down, or a buffet meal?
- Will they provide you with taste samples?
- Can they provide the cake?
- Will you be charged separately for linens, silverware, glassware, and china?
- How many servers and staff members will be provided? How will they dress?
- What time will they need access to the location to set up?

Keep in mind that if you're hiring a caterer for an outdoor affair, you may also need a tent, which is an added cost (and most likely will necessitate your dealing specifically with a tent company).

The Cake

Looking for the perfect wedding cake hardly seems like a chore—they're all so pretty and so perfect, any one will do just fine, you think. The bride, however, has very specific ideas about what she wants and what she *won't* accept, which makes this transaction almost as labor-intensive as finding the right place for the reception.

Ⓔ ALERT!

Take climate into consideration when ordering a cake! No one wants to eat a runny cheesecake or a droopy fruit-filled confection at a patio reception on a hot August day. The cake will look and taste horrible if it melts.

Finding the Right Baker

First of all, you'll need to find someone who specializes in wedding cakes. Yes, your neighbor might be an incredible baker, but this is one confection you don't want to leave to chance. If you don't know of a wedding cake business in the area, ask around. Go to the wedding shows. If all else fails, open the phone book.

Schedule a taste-testing appointment with any prospective baker, because aside from ordering a beautiful cake, you'll want it to be delicious, as well. If the cake is delectable enough, you can serve it for dessert at the reception, thus really getting every penny's worth out of all of those eggs and flour.

Plain or Fancy?

Talk about price before you get into discussing the fanciest cake the baker can muster up for you. A wedding cake is usually priced by the slice, and the price of the slice is based on what it contains. A base price is usually for plain cake with buttercream frosting. As you add to that slice (fillings, upgraded frosting choices, unusual design work), the price rises accordingly. For example, if a plain piece of cake costs $2.50, but your daughter wants a fruit filling and fondant frosting, you'll probably be paying several dollars per piece above the base price. If you need a cake that will feed 300 guests, you're looking at paying well over $1,000 for dessert. (If you have no idea how much cake you'll need, ask the baker. Most will advise serving sizes of three- to four-inch slices. If in doubt, err on the side of caution—you don't want to be short on cake!)

Ⓔ ESSENTIAL

Ask the baker if you can see pictures of cakes from recent weddings; if your daughter has her own ideas, she should bring along a picture or two as well.

If you want your guests to be awed by the cake's sheer magnificence, your baker will have an array of upgrades available for your choosing: different flavored cakes (which might range from chocolate to cherry-macadamia and everything in between); fillings (fruits, cream fillings, or nuts); different toppings (chocolate or fudge sauce, for example); and cakes that really should qualify as art (shaped like gift packages or seashells or anything you can think of, really).

Other matters to discuss when interviewing the baker:

- Is delivery included in the price? What if the reception is outside of the delivery area?
- Can fresh or silk flowers be added to the cake or placed in between the tiers?
- If the cake is destroyed before or during delivery, will another cake be available for the reception? Will there be a price adjustment if it's a less expensive substitution?
- What time will the cake be delivered to the reception site?
- Will you be charged extra for pillars, fountains, or cake supports?

Ⓔ FACT

The Groom's Cake is an old Southern tradition, though Northeners have been known to dig into this confection, as well. This cake is usually less formal, and often whimsically shaped. Consider serving it at the rehearsal dinner, so it won't have to share the spotlight with the wedding cake.

Some receptions include a pastry table (or an entire room filled with goodies) later in the evening, after the guests have worn themselves out boogying. If you're planning on providing the partygoers with a sugar boost, you'll want to know whether this baker can serve up the sweets.

The Pictures

Pictures and videos are one area where brides and grooms are sometimes willing to contribute their monetary resources. Figuring (logically) that after the wedding has come and gone, the images of the event will be what last a lifetime, they want to make sure as many moments as possible from their big day have been captured on film. Finding the right photographer and videographer sometimes takes a bit of effort. You don't automatically want to go with whoever is least expensive, because the discounted price may indicate a lack of experience, and you don't want an amateur shooting the entire day. On the other hand, all good photographers have to work their way up from the bottom, so you may not necessarily need to find someone who has been in the business for thirty years.

Did You Hire *This* Person?

You'll have two choices when looking for a wedding photographer: working with an independent photographer, or working with a studio. (There's actually a third, unadvisable choice, which is hiring a friend or family member to take photos. Unless he or she is a professional photographer, don't do it. If the pictures turn out badly, you'll be forced into a confrontation that will never be resolved, because you and the bride will mourn the loss of those pictures *forever.*)

Ⓔ ALERT!

Good photographers are in high demand. Start looking around as soon as you can, and if you just love someone's work, don't wait to book. His or her schedule will be filled before you know it, and *you'll* end up snapping the wedding pictures with a disposable camera.

There are some differences between an independent photographer and a studio, the biggest one being that an independent one is the person who will show up to take the wedding pictures; with a studio, you may not know who will be entrusted with the task. If you want to work with a particular studio because a friend has recommended the place to you, get the name of the photographer she dealt with. If the studio can't guarantee the same photographer, or even guarantee *any* specific photographer, think about taking your business elsewhere. You want to see this person's work, and you want to know that he or she has experience with weddings. You're paying too much to leave these pictures to chance.

Where *Is* Your Photographer?

How will you find the right photographer? The best way to begin your search is through the recommendations of others. (You already knew that, of course.) Ask recent brides or former MOBs about the photographer that they dealt with. Was he courteous? Prompt? Professional? Did the guests avoid him like the plague, or was he able to develop a rapport with the crowd? (Or was he so unobtrusive that no one even noticed him snapping his brilliant candid shots?) How did the pictures turn out? Were the prices reasonable—and if they were sky-high, was there a discernable reason? (Are the wedding pictures the most amazing shots anyone has ever seen, for example?) Your other best bets: wedding fairs and photography exhibits or art shows.

What to Ask

Of course, after you've narrowed down the choices, you'll have to interview the photographers yourself. You'll want to know how long they've been in business, and what their background or training is. Right off the bat, you should ask these people whether they specialize in weddings or whether they work in a studio; there's a world of difference between the two. One is an *anything-can-happen-and-I'd-better-be-prepared* environment . . . and one is a carefully controlled atmosphere. You don't want this guy's first curveballs to be thrown at him during your daughter's wedding.

What are you looking for in the pictures on display? Quality. Craftsmanship. Creativity. These terms mean nothing to you, you say? Carefully consider the organization of the photos: Do they include a variety of people (the wedding party *and* most of the guests), backgrounds, and activities (posed *and* action shots, candid *and* group shots)? Are all of the important points of any wedding day (the exchange of vows, the triumphant exit from the church, the cake cutting, the toasts, the dancing) captured in the pictures before you?

ⓔ ESSENTIAL

If a photographer hasn't been recommended to you by anyone, ask for references, even if you're very happy with the photos on display. If it takes a year and a half, twenty angry phone calls, and four threatening letters to get the photos delivered . . . maybe you should keep looking.

When considering a package, ask how many pictures the photographer will take. If you're thinking about a fifty-picture package, the bride should end up with about 150 proofs to choose from. You'll also want to know whether you can purchase more pictures after the wedding, and how much those pictures will cost. Be direct in asking about pricing—is it a flat rate plus the photo package, or will you be paying by the hour?

The Video

Videographers are sometimes affiliated with photographers; sometimes, they're independent contractors. (And *how* will you find this person? Yes, through personal recommendations or wedding shows. A photographer can also toss you the name of one or two options.) You'll want to know how many weddings they've filmed, and you'll want to see some of their most recent work. Get some references from them and *call these people*. Ask about the equipment (you should hear the terms *digital* and *DVD* being thrown into the conversation) and editing techniques: Do they include titles in the finished product? How about music or special effects? What does each package include? How many copies can you order and how much will each cost?

The Music

You'll need to entertain your guests before, during, and after the ceremony with music. You may hire separate musicians for the ceremony, the cocktail hour, and the reception, or you may call on the same group to do double (or triple) duty somewhere.

Music for the Ceremony

Are you looking for a soloist, an organist, a string quartet, a guitarist? If this is a church wedding, check with the powers that be first to make sure that the music your daughter wants is allowed (some churches demand that the music during marriage ceremonies be religious;

others allow secular music as long as it meets certain criteria).

 FACT

> The right music passes the time in the interim between when the guests arrive and when the bride makes her entrance; it intensifies the ceremony; and it gets your guests up and shakin' at the reception.

Next . . . you'll need to track down the perfect performers. If your daughter loves organ music and your church already has an organist, your job is fairly easy. However, if she's looking for a topnotch soprano or a professional string quartet for the ceremony, you'll obviously have a bit of work on your hands. You can, of course, go by word of mouth, but if that isn't yielding any candidates, start making the wedding rounds, just to listen to the music. You can simply approach the musicians for their contact information after the ceremony if you like what you hear.

Reception Music

For most brides and grooms (and MOBs), the question of the reception music comes down to two choices: a band or a DJ. Some people find that they have a strong preference from the get-go, and would never consider the alternative, while other folks really try to weigh the pros and cons of each.

Even if someone gives you the name of the best band or DJ in town, it's important for you to hear them before you go ahead and sign a contract with them. Picture the guests who will be at your reception and ask yourself if they will enjoy the type of music you're listening to (if the guest list is heavy on the younger crowd, and all you're hearing are old standards, the reception could fizzle out very early in the evening). How does the band leader or DJ handle his emcee responsibilities? Is he hijacking the evening by practicing his lame stand-up routine? Is he dignified enough for your crowd of friends and relatives? What about his apparel (and that of the band)?

 FACT

Generally speaking, a live band is perceived as being a bit classier; DJs are completely acceptable at a formal reception, however, and you'll find that hiring a man with a sound system is going to be less expensive than bringing in a four or five piece band.

Of course, if you like what you're hearing, but the playlist isn't quite perfect for your daughter's wedding, there's a chance that the band or DJ has an entirely different set which is appropriate for other occasions. If you're almost won over, take the time to schedule an interview and discuss other options. A good band (or DJ) is not always easy to find, and since the best guys are booked more than a year in advance, this is not a task you want to leave unfinished for too long.

Depending on the size of the wedding, you may have a fairly easy time whipping up the guest list, or you may find yourself making precise, surgical cuts here and there—and encouraging the groom's family to do the same. If this is a second wedding, you may not know whether it's appropriate to invite the same guests you mingled with at your daughter's first marriage. And then there's the small matter of purchasing and *assembling* the invitations, which should really be covered in a college-level course somewhere.

One for You, and One for Me . . .

Even if the groom's family isn't taking on a large part of the wedding expenses, they are entitled to invite their friends and relatives to the reception—and they should be allowed to invite roughly as many guests as your family is inviting. Remember, when all is said and done, this is a celebration of your daughter's and their son's marriage, and the groom's parents will want to have their loved ones in attendance, too.

Years ago, the guest list was split evenly between the two families, which made for an easy time of conjuring up the magical number of attendees for each side. However, with more and more couples paying for their own weddings these days, and because more brides and grooms are waiting until they're older to walk down the aisle (and hence have their own group of friends and business associates they might like to include at the reception), the guest list is sometimes split three ways now: One-third of the head count goes to the bride and groom; a third goes to the bride's family; and the remaining third goes to the groom's family. Everyone's happy, and no one can be accused of commandeering the entire guest list.

Who's In, Who's Out

Before you can even think of drawing up a list of potential reception revelers, you need to think about who should be invited—and who shouldn't. Each family is different, of course, but there are some general guidelines you might want to follow, and some advice that may help you out of some pretty hot water down the line. The first thing you need to know is this: If you're hosting a large reception, *someone* is going to be offended at not being invited or be unhappy about *being* invited. Unfortunately, this is the nature of the wedding season. You can't please everyone, not even when you try your hardest to do so.

The Family

Obviously, if the reception is a small affair, you'll have to pick and choose between extended family members very carefully. Only those people who have (recently) been very close to you or your daughter would *expect* to be invited to such an intimate gathering. If you're limited to twenty spaces, you'll have to pick and choose your guests very carefully—and wisely. (In other words, don't feel badly about not being able to invite your best friend from high school, whom you haven't spoken to in several years.)

Many MOBs invite the entire family—aunts, uncles, fourth and fifth cousins, and folks who are only rumored to be blood relatives. Before you go this route, examine your motives. Perhaps your family is huge but extremely close, and by not inviting *everyone*, you'd be breaking the family code of togetherness. Your heart is in the right place if this is your major concern. If, on the other hand, you want a packed house for the sake of appearances ("Look how popular we are! Look how everyone loves our daughter enough to show up!"), you're not fooling anyone, especially if this is your regular modus operandi. All the guests there will know why they were invited—if they bother to show at all.

Ⓔ QUESTION

Should children be invited to a formal wedding?

It's absolutely fine to include close relatives, like nephews and nieces. You might also want to consider a cut-off age for kids—but *stick to it*. Don't include your eight-year-old relative and then tell the groom's mom that her ten-year-old nephew is too young.

Inviting people you hardly know to your daughter's wedding can be construed as a request for gifts. Many families *do* operate this way; there's a tacit rule of reciprocity there (you bought cousin Jane's daughter a lovely set of candlesticks for her wedding; now it's Jane's turn to pony up), and that's fine. When you start inviting distant relations and long-lost friends who aren't in on this exchange system, though, it's more likely that they'll ask themselves how they made it onto the guest list in the first place.

The Associates

Who hasn't been invited to a business associate's wedding or the wedding of a colleague's child at one time or another? Business relationships can be peculiar—you may work with some people you feel extremely close to, but in the same office, there may be folks you barely talk to. Still, you have to work with *all* of these people every day. You certainly don't want to offend anyone, but you also don't want to come across looking as though you're inviting everyone under the sun so that they'll send your daughter a gift. (This invitation thing is *very* tricky.)

The level of difficulty of this situation really depends on how large your workplace is. If your office has 150 people in it, you obviously can't invite everyone, so you're free to include only those you're closest to. If you work in an office of ten employees, though, inviting only six of those people will greatly offend the others—quite possibly for years to come.

 FACT

Don't forget to include the bride's attendants and their guests in your final guest count. You also need to include the parents of any children attendants (because you don't want to end up chasing a wild-child flower girl around the reception hall all night).

Aside from leaving certain coworkers out in the cold, the very issue of a wedding can cause problems in the workplace, wherein the invitees talk in hushed tones about what they're going to wear to the reception, then clam up the second a noninvitee enters the area. Your safest bet in this case is to either invite everyone or to invite no one.

Everybody Else

Should you really invite the entire neighborhood, your hairdresser, the guy who's been plowing your driveway every winter for the past twenty years, your doctor, the mailman, and your accountant? Only if any of them happen to be close friends of yours or of the family. None of these people (or others like them), who are in your life without really being in *on* it, will expect an invitation—or at least they *shouldn't*—even if your small talk with them has consisted of nothing *but* wedding details lately. Most of them would probably find an invitation to your daughter's wedding odd, to say the least.

Guests?

There's been a debate raging for eons as to whether brides should allow their guests to bring guests no matter what the circumstances, or whether each bride should make that decision based on the size and location of her own wedding. A guest's spouse or fiancé should always be included. Of course, now that many couples live together for years before they become officially engaged or married (if they *ever* take those steps), the question of inviting a guest's significant other has become more complicated. Consider couples who live together to be as good as engaged, and include both of them on the guest list.

Ⓔ ESSENTIAL

A single female who is expected to travel to the wedding should be permitted to bring a companion along. Even in this age of independence, some women don't feel comfortable traveling alone. Don't put her well-being at risk for the sake of saving a few bucks on the reception bill.

The Second Wedding

You're planning another wedding for your daughter, and tradition be darned, she wants another big affair. Her reasoning is that while this may be her second trip to the altar, it's her fiancé's first, and he wants a big wedding. She doesn't want her side of the church to be empty, and she wants to see lots of friendly, familiar faces at the reception, so she wants you to break out that address book and invite the usual suspects—again. Is this proper etiquette? Is it any of your business?

The Rule

Etiquette states that a second wedding should be a smaller event than the first one was. As stated in Chapter 7, this rule has its basis in morality, wherein it's deemed inappropriate for a bride or groom to flout broken marriage vows and replace them with newer, hopefully better promises to someone else. While many people (perhaps some of your potential guests, even) may agree with this notion, this dictate came about in the age when second marriages were nothing less than scandalous. Nowadays, just about everybody has a human face to put with the word "remarriage," which has lessened the shock factor of the term considerably.

Still, this is a case-by-case scenario. Some folks tend to have a very rigid view of marriage and remarriage—and if this isn't the bride's first time down the aisle, she's likely to be judged by certain groups as being either morally corrupt or a dingbat. Or both. Bottom line here: If your entire family can best be described as *pious*, forget about inviting them to the second wedding. Your daughter will spend the day under their moral microscopes, if they decide to come at all.

To Invite or Not to Invite?

So you know the official line of etiquette on the guest list for second weddings. You neither agree nor disagree, and you don't know what you should do. Where do you go from here? *You* are the best judge of your guests' reaction to being invited to a big second wedding. Will they gossip over the decision to have another big wedding? Will they come? Will they be angry at being expected to give another gift?

If you really have no problem with the situation but you're a little leery about the guests' reaction, remember the advice that was given at the beginning of this chapter: You'll *never* make everyone happy with the wedding guest list—not even for a first wedding. Sometimes, the only thing you can do is to put yourself on the line. Those who are going to be judgmental will be (and they would be even if they weren't invited to the wedding), and those who want to wish the couple well will. You can't intervene and force everyone to accept the invitation and/or the marriage, so send the invitations and let the rest take care of itself.

Ⓔ FACT

If you're uncomfortable inviting the entire family to another large wedding, don't do it. If she's bound and determined to invite them anyway, the bride can pay for the wedding herself and put her own name and the groom's on the invitations as sponsors.

Former Family Members

Should the bride's ex-in-laws be invited to a second wedding? Probably not. If your daughter's very best friend in the world happens to be her ex-husband's sister, you can make an exception to this rule, but otherwise, keep the exes out of it. It's just not all that common for a bride to remain close to her former in-laws, for one thing, but for another thing, how will the *new* groom's family react to being forced to mingle with the former groom's kin?

(E) ALERT!

No matter how progressive people are, they're bound to question the wisdom of inviting former family to a second wedding. It may seem like a good idea—or at least a harmless idea—but grouping the bride's ex-in-laws with her new ones is probably not wise.

Not every second marriage is the result of divorce, however. If your daughter is a widow and is planning to remarry, she may have some questions as to what's proper and what isn't. The rule for remarriage after death is the same—a smaller affair this time around, out of respect for her deceased husband.

Should the bride invite her late husband's in-laws? If she's remained close to them, she should. Ideally, they should hear about the wedding from her before they receive an invitation in the mail. If she hasn't spoken to these folks in ages, she really doesn't need to include them in the guest list; it just wouldn't make any sense to do so.

The B List

Because many reception facilities and caterers will demand a minimum number of guests (or charge you for uneaten meals), and because many brides love big weddings with lots and lots of onlookers, guest lists sometimes grow like mushrooms—to the point where the bride (or the MOB) is able to make an A list and a B list. The A list contains the names of the people the bride really, really wants at her reception—and the B list is filled with the names of guests who will do if her favorite folks can't make it. Is this a safe plan, or a scheme fraught with peril?

Ⓔ ESSENTIAL

> Thinking of shifting the invites earlier? You won't be fooling anyone. Most people have also been invited to other weddings at some point, and will wonder why your daughter's invitations are the only ones to demand such an early response.

It's a rude plan, really. Wedding invitations are supposed to be mailed a minimum of six weeks before the wedding, with a requested response time of two weeks prior to the event. These time frames can be shifted only *slightly* (the invites can go out as early as eight weeks prior, and the responses can be requested three weeks before the wedding). Anyone who has any inkling of wedding invitation etiquette and receives an invitation a month before the event is going to know that they weren't on the original guest list.

In the end, some of your B list invitees are bound to figure out the game, no matter how skilled you are in trying to pull it off. Before you do a tango with two guest lists, prepare yourself for the possible consequences. Let's say, for example, that your irritating cousin Darla calls to ask why she has only just received her invitation to your daughter's wedding, when she knows darn well that your favorite cousin, Marla, received hers several weeks ago. The jig is up at this point. She already knows what's going on, and she's forcing you to either be brutally honest or to fabricate some sort of fib . . . which is going to sound incredibly lame. (The fact that Darla has the nerve to call you and request an explanation justifies your decision to leave her off the original list, but that's an entirely different discussion.)

Be *very* careful if you're dealing with an A list and a B list. Your intention (hopefully) is not to insult your relatives; however, because weddings tend to illuminate *everyone's* true colors (including deep-seated issues of insecurity . . . and the ability to hold grudges), you may suffer the consequences of hurt feelings for years to come. If you can't handle the fallout, it may be best to bite the bullet and invite everyone . . . or to cut the guest list among definitive lines (e.g., first cousins are in, second cousins are out).

Selecting the Invitations

Drawing up the guest list is only the beginning of what often proves to be a labor-intensive process. Unless your daughter knows exactly what she wants in the way of invites, the two of you will be faced with oodles of choices, from the paper to the ink to the printing process and style.

Assembling the invitations and addressing them may require you to recruit an army of helpers—and *then*, you'll deal with acceptances (yeah!) and regrets (boo!) and guests who simply fail to respond (double boo!).

 FACT

It may be easier to deal with a store in town should you have any problems with the invitations down the line. No matter how good the customer service department of an Internet site may be, a nervous bride may need the reassurance of a human being she can actually *see*.

Where to Get Invitations

Many wedding planners start their search for the invitations at a printer or a shop (stationery or department store) that offers printing services. These days, the Internet also offers a wide array of choices for those who are comfortable shopping in cyberspace. Unless you are a veritable expert in printing methods and paper, though, you may be better off hitting a shop (at least initially), where you can actually see what the invitations will look and feel like once they're finished.

Invitation catalogs are filled with sample invites that can be customized for your daughter's wedding. Often, she'll have to pick a color, a script style, and a printing method—but the rest of the invitation (the design, the phrasing) is duplicated in the final product. It's a fairly easy process for any bride to get through. If she's looking for something more unique, she may want to visit a print shop and talk to a designer on the premises. She can throw out her ideas and work with the store to create an invitation that suits her specific ideas. Be aware that this will cost more than ordering the invitations out of a catalog.

Technical Stuff

There are several printing methods to choose from, and this choice will affect the final cost of the invitations. *Engraving* is the most expensive (and elegant) option, so if your daughter has her heart set on the fanciest invitations in town, you may be paying through the nose for them—then again, you may not have to. *Thermography* is another option. It produces a raised-letter print that is almost identical to engraving, but at a much lower price.

Many brides love the look of *calligraphy*; however, hiring a calligrapher to produce hundreds of invitations might not be the most financially-friendly idea. More good news: Printers now have access to computer software that can simulate handscripted calligraphy at a fraction of the price of hiring a human to do the same job.

Ⓔ **ESSENTIAL**

> Wording the invitation can be a tricky little task: If there is more than one host, or the hosts have divorced each other and remarried, how will the invitation reflect this? And how is a *traditional* invitation worded, anyway? Don't worry—see Appendix B for guidelines and samples.

Little Extras

Some wedding invitations arrive packed with little inserts. Love 'em or hate 'em, sometimes they're the best way to let your guests in on certain information. Consider your options:

Ceremony cards. If the wedding is being held in a public place (a museum, for example), you want your guests to be able to scoot past those who are waiting in line to pay admission.

Pew cards (or "Within the Ribbon" cards). Slip these cards into the appropriate invitations if you're planning on reserving the front section of the church for special guests (usually family and the closest friends).

The guests will then give them to the ushers, who will seat them in the reserved area.

Rain cards. These cards alert guests to an alternate location if the wedding site could be affected by inclement weather.

Response cards and envelopes. The card includes the date of the requested RSVP; the envelope will have a preprinted return address.

Reception cards. Although you'll be offered the option of printing the reception information on the wedding invitation itself, it's classier to have a separate insert.

Envelopes. Do they need to be foil-lined? No. Ask yourself where the envelopes end up (think *trashcan*), and go with the less expensive options.

Thank-yous. Most often, the bride and groom will order cards that complement the wedding invitations. Their married names are usually printed on these cards (whether it's Mr. and Mrs. James Smith *or* Allison Brown and James Smith).

Putting It All Together

You should order the invitations and all the accompanying inserts a minimum of four months before the wedding—not only so that they will have plenty of time to arrive, but because you'll also need time to put them together into little packages for your guests' enjoyment. When you pick up your order, you'll have everything you ordered—plus tissue paper and envelopes. What goes where and why?

If the invitation is folded, the inserts go inside of the first fold; if the invites are one flat sheet, the inserts go on top—either way, they go in this order: tissue paper (on top of the printing on the invitation, so that it doesn't smudge), reception card, map, response envelope, response card under the flap of its envelope. All of this goes inside the ungummed inner envelope with the printed side of the invitation facing the flap.

Ⓔ ALERT!

Don't forget the stamps for the reply cards! Have one weighed at the post office to make sure it's standard size, shape, and weight—or you may need extra postage.

Those inner envelopes need to be addressed, too, which is where many brides and MOBs run into difficulty if they're trying to adhere to etiquette standards. So many issues crop up here: Should proper titles be used? Does an entire family living in one house receive one all-purpose invitation?

Addressing the Envelopes

First of all, if you know the guest in question well, you're free to be as informal as you wish on the inner envelope. If your brother is an M.D., there's no need to address him as Doctor Nolan here—you can simply use his first name. On the other hand, if Dr. Nolan is not a close personal friend, you'd keep his title as-is. Be aware that professional titles undergo a metamorphosis when they're moved from the outer envelope to the inner one. See the following chart for some examples:

| Invitation Envelope Etiquette | |
Outer Envelope	Inner Envelope
Lawyer	
Mitchell Nolan, Esq.	Mr. Nolan
Physician	
Ann Nolan, M.D.	Doctor Nolan
	(or Doctor Ann Nolan)
Married Physicians	
Doctors Mitchell and	The Doctors Nolan
Ann Nolan	
Married Male Physician	
Doctor and	Doctor Nolan and
Mrs. Mitchell Nolan	Mrs. Nolan
Married Female Physician	
Doctor Ann Nolan and	Doctor Nolan
Mr. Mitchell Nolan	and Mr. Nolan
PhD.	
Dr. Mitchell Nolan	Dr. Nolan
Minister	
The Reverend	The Reverend Nolan
Mitchell Nolan	
Catholic Priest	
Father Mitchell Nolan	Father Nolan
Rabbi	
Rabbi Mitchell Nolan	Rabbi Nolan
Judge	
The Honorable Ann Nolan	Judge Nolan

Most of these titles allow a spouse to be tacked on fairly easily, such as in the case of The Honorable and Mrs. Mitchell Nolan, or The Reverend and Mrs. Mitchell Nolan. Small children, meanwhile, are not even acknowledged on the outer envelope, which is addressed to their parents; the inner envelope will have only the children's first names listed according to age under their parents' names.

 FACT

> Before you send one invitation to an entire family, make sure any children who are included are under eighteen; if they're older, they should be sent their own invitation, even if their address is exactly the same as their parents'.

Other rules to follow: Titles are used in conjunction with first names on the outer envelope; the first names are dropped on the inner envelope. In the case of Miss Ann Thompson (addressed as such on the outer envelope), the inner envelope would read "Miss Thompson." In the case of an unmarried, cohabiting couple (or a same-gender couple), their names are listed in alphabetical order, like so: Outer envelope—Mr. Mitchell Nolan, Miss Ann Thompson. Inner envelope—Mr. Nolan, Miss Thompson.

"And Guest"

The phrase "and guest" stirs up more trouble than it should. Followers of rigid etiquette rules frown upon these two little words (as in "Mr. Mitchell Nolan and guest"). The *proper* way to go about this is to find out the name of the guest's guest and to issue her a separate invitation. This requires an extraordinary amount of time and effort, especially if you don't know the primary guest very well in the first place. (Will you really feel comfortable calling a distant relative to ask whether he's dating anyone special—oh, and by the way, could you have her name and address?)

No one will fault you for tacking "and guest" onto the names in the inner envelopes. It's done every day, for weddings formal and informal, and is becoming more and more standard practice. It's very *kind* of you to let your guests invite their own guests to your daughter's wedding; leave it at that and move on.

Responses

MOBs and brides alike love to run to the mailbox and gather up the responses to the wedding invitations. Organize a checklist with the names of the invitees, so that you'll be able to easily tally a final head count for the caterer. If a guest simply fails to respond, don't be shy about making a phone call. There's no need to be snippy with the errant invitee, though. It's possible that this person forgot all about sending the response card, or just didn't realize the etiquette surrounding it.

Chapter 10

Where and How to Save Money

U p till this point, this book has focused on some basic wedding planning issues: how to get organized, how to design a strategy for successful communications with all of the interested parties, how to find the right dress and the right caterer, etc. If money is no object, all of this will be a relative breeze for you. The MOB who is forced to pinch pennies, however, will emerge from the planning process feeling either exhausted or triumphant. The difference? Creativity.

The Ground Rules

You already know that when you're working with a budget, the bride and groom need to prioritize their needs (and because all they really *need* to get married is a marriage license and an officiant, they'll really be prioritizing wants—no matter how badly the bride feels she *needs* a $2,000 gown, that's a want). Before doing anything else, make a list of what's most important to the two of them. Include both the bride and the groom in this discussion, so that you won't later be accused of being insensitive to your future son-in-law's wishes. Present them with the total budget, so that they both have some idea of how much money is in the wedding kitty. If neither of them has previously demonstrated any understanding of the value of a dollar, this may be a great learning experience for them—both for the wedding planning and for the real life that follows.

Picking Favorites

Once their top choices have been laid out, the bride and groom then have the option to try to include the less important items or vendors, or to leave them out all together. You should encourage them to make wise choices here without taking over the list yourself. For example, if your daughter has talked about nothing but the flowers since she got engaged, and is willing to cut back on everything else in the name of dispersing blossoms and buds all over the church and reception area (where very little food will be served, by the way, because all of the money went to the pretty decorations), encourage her to rethink this decision.

Ⓔ ESSENTIAL

Remember: Your guests' comfort (i.e., food and drink) should be taken into consideration when planning the wedding budget—or else they shouldn't be invited. Lovely decorations and the best music are small comforts to people who are searching in vain for *anything* edible during the reception.

Give Yourself the Gift of Time

Every item on the list is fair game for creative price cuts. Be forewarned: This cost-cutting is a commitment. This is not something that can be successfully achieved over a three-day period. But it's possible to pull off a classy, *relatively* inexpensive wedding if you get to work on the planning early enough. Getting a late start almost guarantees that you're going to pay too much for something, or that the final event will look shoddy.

Even if your daughter is planning a long engagement (a year and a half or more), don't give in to the urge to procrastinate (even if this is a primal urge for you). Don't tell yourself, "I work best under pressure"; don't allow yourself to believe that the most creative parties aren't planned—they just *happen*. You may have planned hundreds of parties in your home this way, and all of them may have gone off without a hitch. Wedding planning is a completely different undertaking. You need to get with the program early on, *especially* if you're looking to save some money.

Free Your Mind, Mom

You and your daughter may have some very definite visions for her wedding. When you're looking to cut costs, it's all right to maintain those visions, but it's just as important to be flexible and open-minded. A florist may have some incredibly creative, low-cost ideas to present to the two of you, but if you go into that shop thinking, "Nosegays. Nothing but nosegays," you're severely limiting any assistance that can be rendered you.

ⓔ ALERT!

Be willing to listen to a vendor's ideas. If you're unwilling to bend, you'll end up getting exactly what you wanted—but you won't have saved a dime. Who knows—the alternate suggestion may have been the less expensive *and* more beautiful option.

When you're trying to save money on a wedding, *ask* for help from the experts, and *listen* to their suggestions.

People who work in the wedding industry are usually accustomed to dealing with different-sized budgets; they know the current trends; they also often know how to fake those trends using less expensive materials. Remember, these folks answer wedding-related questions on a daily basis; don't be afraid to ask for their help. They won't think you're the cheapest person on the planet—they'll think you're just like the last MOB who walked through their doors (and the one before her, and the one before *her*).

Flower Power

It's no secret to anyone who's ever purchased flowers as a gift for someone else, or who loves to decorate their home with fresh flowers: They're expensive. You'd like to think that buying in bulk—say, for a wedding—would cut down on the cost of the little buds, but you'll find that the size of your bank account is the only thing reduced by purchasing gads of roses and lilies. Are you simply doomed, then, to spend more than you'd like on this aspect of your daughter's big day? No, ma'am. There are many ways to ensure that your daughter's wedding is beautifully decorated without diving headfirst into debt.

Finding the Florist

Start shopping around for the right florist at least four months prior to the wedding—earlier than that if you have the time. You'll want to compare services, creativity, and prices of various florists, and you'll also want to give yourself ample opportunity to see their work at local weddings, receptions, or other events.

When you make an appointment to meet with the florist, have a solid concept of what you're willing to spend. A creative florist will have ideas for any budget; indeed, most florists can correctly be called artists. A florist who is in the business primarily to gouge customers will show you arrangements that are obviously above and beyond your means, and in that case, you should take your business elsewhere. This person is wasting your time in the hopes of pushing you to spend more. Another florist—one who will actually listen to what you're saying—is waiting for you. You just have to find him or her. Be persistent. (This is when you'll be glad you gave yourself plenty of time.)

 FACT

Finding a good florist is as easy as remembering where your long-lasting bouquet of roses came from last Valentine's Day, or by asking friends for recommendations. You can also ask other wedding vendors, such as your banquet manager or photographer, whom they would recommend.

Are They Real, or Are They . . . *Not?*

One popular suggestion for saving money on wedding flowers is to use silk instead of fresh cuts. If silk flowers are done well, they can look real; however, there's an overabundance of fake-looking silk out there, so you do have to choose carefully, and it's best not to enter into this project alone. Take a brutally honest friend or relative along on the silk-flower hunt. If she tells you she's never seen a blue daisy in all of her life, and incorporating the silk variety of this flower into your daughter's wedding will be tacky, listen to her.

Good silks are going to be less expensive than fresh flowers; however, the best (and most realistic) silk flowers are not going to be as cheap as you might think (or hope). Do the math before you order or purchase silk arrangements. If you're making the concession to silk strictly because you expect it to be a far less expensive option, ask yourself if you could substitute smaller bouquets of fresh flowers for the same price as larger silk arrangements. The price may end up being comparable.

On the other hand, silk lasts forever, and if you and the bride are planning on recycling her wedding arrangements and using them in your home decor, this is obviously a cost-effective and wise purchase for that reason alone.

Wholesalers will sometimes offer the same services as an independent florist (arrangements, delivery, wiring or taping the bouquets) but for less money. Internet companies can offer low, low prices on their products, along with how-to instructions for assembling the floral arrangements for the wedding. If you're fairly confident that you can handle the care and delivery of the flowers (to the church and to the reception site) on the day of the wedding, this may be a viable option for you. Look carefully at the site's delivery policy. When will the flowers arrive, and how? Is there a contingency plan in case the truck or plane carrying your order doesn't arrive? You don't want to be left searching for flowers—*any* flowers—on your way to the church.

Ⓔ ESSENTIAL

Think about a compromise. If your daughter just has to have that fresh-flower smell at her wedding, have a mixture of real flowers where they're most important—in the bouquets, in the centerpieces—and silk flowers (or other less expensive options) where fresh flowers won't be missed.

Common Sense

When the bride is sighing over the gorgeous orchids in the flower shop, pull her away to look at something else—anything else, in fact. Orchids (and roses) tend to be among the most expensive floral options. Steer her towards flowers that are in season and widely available in your area; while almost any flower can be made available for a wedding, out-of-season and exotic blooms will cost you much more. In-season flowers also tend to accentuate the wedding itself: If your daughter is getting married in December, wouldn't it be lovely and appropriate to incorporate poinsettias in the overall design of the wedding flowers—instead of trying to dredge up some sunflowers?

And speaking of holidays . . . Christmas and Easter are *wonderful* times for saving money on wedding flowers, because most churches are already decorated for these seasons. Valentine's Day, conversely, is one of the most expensive holidays to get married on or around; flower prices are routinely jacked up in the weeks preceding February 14.

More tips for saving money on the flowers:

• The bride can cut her number of attendants. Having ten bridesmaids means that she will shell out for ten bouquets (and most likely ten boutonnieres).

• A single flower dramatized with a ribbon is just as lovely for the bridesmaids to carry as a huge nosegay is.

• A wedding in an already decorated setting (think public garden or museum) needs very little in the way of decorations.

• Grocery store florists are usually much cheaper than their independent counterparts. Be prepared to *really* investigate this option, though, to make sure the flowers are of the best quality.

• Splitting the cost of the church flowers can save you a bundle: Ask the minister if another wedding is scheduled for the same day, and contact the other bride.

And just remember what some men love to tell their significant others: Flowers die. Of course, these men are also likely to follow that phrase with, "No use spending good money on them." That sentiment doesn't exactly hold true here—a wedding might end up looking a little sad without a few blossoms to perk things up. However, you could wind up feeling downright morose if you discover too late that you could have spent much, much less on the decorations. Give yourself plenty of time and explore all of your floral options.

Ⓔ ALERT!

Keep in mind that holiday weddings often carry higher price tags for other services, such as catering, photography, and the like. You may find that you can eliminate the cost of flowers for the church because it's already been decorated, but you shouldn't expect to find many bargains elsewhere.

Dressing Up the Reception

If the reception is being held in a location without a single decoration, you could conceivably spend a fortune on simply making the place look less barren. A great option for dressing up plain halls is to call some local nurseries and ask them if they rent out potted plants. Put them in the corners, place them in the entryway, pop one next to the head table. If you're not completely sold on this idea, thinking that everything will just look too green and dark, consider stringing some clear "twinkle" lights on the plants. There's just something dreamy and whimsical about little lights that echo stars in the sky—or fireflies in the yard.

 FACT

Some brides opt for simple, fresh floral centerpieces—and are still able to meet their budget. Consider small bud vases at each table, or candles surrounded by fresh petals.

Candles are another less expensive option for beautifying a reception hall on the cheap. You'll find candles come in all sizes and colors, and are much, *much* cheaper than floral centerpieces. Float a candle in a crystal bowl; you'll be amazed at the light it gives off. Slide a mirror underneath and the effect is even lovelier. (You can also do different centerpieces at different tables. Have fresh flowers at half and candles at the other half.) Make sure to ask your banquet manager if the use of candles is permitted in his facility. Hurricane lamps are often an option if the flames must be covered.

The Dresses

While the bride should be encouraged to take pity on her attendants and choose a dress that each of them can actually afford, in the end, this is not really *your* problem. Neither you nor the bride will be responsible for the cost of the bridesmaids' dresses. You'll be looking for your own dress, and helping the bride to find her best look. Some brides (and MOBs) opt to put their dress near the top of their financial priority list, thinking that they'll be on display all day, and they only get to buy this kind of dress once, so they might as well go all out. While this may be true . . . there *are* ways to dress to kill without killing your wallet in the process.

Take Your Time

Starting early is, of course, going to make things easier on you when you're looking for your own dress, and is going to give the bride lots of time to mull things over when she's looking for hers. If she decides to order through a dress shop, she'll need to do so at least six months prior to the wedding, so the sooner she gets moving on the search for the perfect wedding fashion statement, the better.

Encourage her to explore all avenues before she decides on a dress. If she's dead set against buying a gown through a bridal store, she should start looking for a dress as soon as the ring hits her finger. Sure, it takes less time to purchase an off-the-rack dress from a boutique or department store . . . but if she doesn't find anything there, and she's only started looking a couple of months before the wedding, she's going to be in a real pickle.

Ⓔ FACT

Skip the bridal shop bras. The bride does not need to buy undergarments from the bridal shop. A crinoline may be hard to come by elsewhere, but strapless bras and girdles—and shoes—can be found in any mall, and at much lower prices than at a bridal store.

Hunting for Bargains

Obviously, buying a gown at a bridal warehouse is going to be cheaper than buying that same dress through a bridal shop; that's why prospective brides place themselves in the middle of the competitive atmospheres that are par for the course at some of these shops. One word of advice you should offer to her: Cheap is good; flattering is *mandatory*. She might snag a designer dress at a rock-bottom price, but if it doesn't look good on her, the money she's spent on it is a waste. No one will be reading the tag of her dress, after all, or *oohing* and *ahhing* over the designer of the gown; guests will either be in awe of the bride's beauty (if she has chosen a complementary dress) or confused as to why she chose a gown that doesn't suit her at all.

If she'd rather not slog her way through the racks in the warehouses, she might opt to visit the local bridal shops. Are there bargains to be found here, or should the two of you resign yourself to paying full price for any dress within the confines of those walls? You could get lucky and find a real deal—but you may also have to *ask* for the specials. Bridal stores run end-of-season discount sales; sometimes they have off-the-rack sample gowns for sale. Sales are usually advertised; the leftovers from these sales may sit until someone specifically comes looking for them.

Ⓔ ESSENTIAL

The bride who's looking to save a buck on her dress may want to start by asking friends and relatives if she can borrow their old wedding gowns. Most women have their dresses stored away somewhere, and would be honored to be of assistance in this manner.

A bride who is looking for something a little less formal might find the perfect dress in the bridesmaids' racks. Some of these dresses are very elegant and are available in ivory—at much lower prices than the typical wedding dress. If your daughter is pursuing this option, she should also take a look in department stores and boutiques for evening gowns that could double as wedding wear.

Here Comes the Dress . . . Again

While many brides are insistent on having the dress of their dreams, to have and to hold (in a box in their closet) from this day forward, others see the logic in spending far less for the dress they'll wear for one day, and then pack away. These brides don't even care if their dress is brand-new, which opens up another world of opportunity for them.

Bridal consignment shops specialize in recycling wedding dresses. If your daughter is in the market for a used dress, she can pop into one of these stores and browse around. If there's nothing to her liking (or nothing that fits), the storeowner can keep her eyes peeled for something that meets the description your daughter has given her.

Rental shops are one way to *really* keep costs low. Some bridal shops offer rental gowns, while some shops send their older gowns out to be rented. If you and the bride are dealing with a bridal shop but are thinking about renting, ask the owner about these other options.

Renting a gown has its disadvantages, however. The bride will be choosing from a smaller selection of dresses (which is also one disadvantage to shopping in consignment stores); also, many shops won't do extensive alterations on their rental dresses, so the gown may not fit her as well as a purchased dress would.

Is it wise to buy a dress online, either through an auction, or a designer or shop's Web site? These dresses may be incredibly cheap, but the bride obviously can't try them on; it's also likely that she won't be able to return a dress that just doesn't fit. (Though she can, of course, resell the gown if need be.) If she can handle the possible negative outcomes of this transaction, it may be worth her time and effort.

 **QUESTION**

What about saving money on the mother of the bride dress?
Your options are very similar to the bride's. Start early and keep an open mind. Ask for discounts. Look for sales. Ask your friends about borrowing their MOB dresses. Consider renting. Above all, make sure you look stunning in whatever you choose.

The Bar Tab

Prepare yourself: The bar bill for the reception can end up being astronomical. The very thought of paying top-dollar for liquor sends some wedding sponsors into a mode of stinginess unparalleled by even the most stringent bean counters. Should you opt for a cash bar instead, or make it a "dry" reception? Rest assured, there are some ways to provide your guests with alcohol without going broke.

Cash Bar or Open Bar?

First things first; if you're inviting adult guests to a wedding, you need to provide them with food and drink. This means you have to shell out for some kind of liquor. It's just rude to ask your friends and relatives to attend the ceremony, to bring a gift to the reception . . . oh, and to pay for their own beer or wine or martinis, too. Unless the consumption of alcohol is against your religious or moral beliefs (and no fair converting *now* just to save yourself some money), accept the fact that you're going to have to face the bar bill. That being said, you don't have to make an open bar an extravagant, bank-breaking free-for-all. There are plenty of ways to open the bar on a fairly limited basis, while still maintaining the appearance of being extremely generous to your guests.

Ⓔ ESSENTIAL

One of the most obvious ways to cut down the cost of alcohol—and many other wedding expenses—is to simply keep the guest count low. Start cutting back on that number, and suddenly, the reception bill takes a dive, along with the cost of the invitations.

Early Birds

If you're still in the earliest planning phases, and the bride hasn't yet reserved the church or the reception hall, one of the best ways to cut back on the consumption of alcohol during the reception is to time it correctly. Think about it: When do most people start drinking? With dinner, or in the early evening. Move the ceremony to the morning; follow it with a reception brunch or an early-afternoon lunch. During a brunch, you'll still want to include a champagne or sparkling wine toast (or perhaps substitute mimosas, a.k.a., champagne diluted with orange juice); for an early-afternoon affair, you may want to include wine and beer in the open bar, or you might be able to substitute a champagne punch, which will lower your liquor cost substantially.

 FACT

Early receptions save you money. Your food and bar bills will be significantly lower than they would be for an evening soiree. You won't need to feed your guests dinner, which is by far the most expensive meal in most reception facilities.

Cut It Back

If the bride has her little heart set on an evening reception, all hope is not lost. You can still control the amount (and type) of alcohol flowing from the bar into your guests' bloodstreams, but you'll need to know what's permitted in the reception hall and what isn't. Some ideas for your consideration (and to present to the banquet manager):

Tray service. Have the servers carry trays of champagne and wine for a limited time. You're providing the guests with booze, but not for the entire evening. Expect to see fewer drunken guests than you would with a completely open bar.

Limit the drinks. Offer beer, wine, and a cocktail matching the wedding's colors. (The bridesmaids are wearing blue? Blue Hawaiians should hit the spot.)

Nix the champagne toast. Very few people actually *choose* to drink champagne. Have the guests toast the bride and groom with whatever they happen to be drinking at the time, or substitute a less expensive sparkling wine for an "official" toast.

Keep in mind that many upscale reception facilities charge an enormous mark up on liquor—so don't be shy about asking if you can supply your own alcohol. You'll probably be charged a corkage fee, but you can bet your bottom dollar that it will be less than paying for an open bar on the premises. (In some cases, the corkage fee can be whittled down, anyway.)

Case by Case (by Case)

In the event that you are permitted to bring your own liquor to the reception, you'll need to know how much booze to buy. There must be some sort of mathematical equation out there for such an event, something your high school trigonometry teacher covered (complete with graphs), but that you just can't seem to recall . . . If x is equal to the number of guests you're serving, then *y* must equal the amount of alcohol you'll need . . . ?

Not exactly, but you *can* come pretty darn close to the right amount. Figure that each *adult* guest (here's where you go through the guest list and subtract any children from your head count—for now) will average four to five drinks over the course of an evening reception (some will drink more, of course, but some won't drink at all).

(E) ESSENTIAL

Ask your liquor store about their return policy. You may already have plans for any leftover liquor, but if it's going to go to waste (or sit in your basement storage room forever), you might be able to return unopened bottles of wine and liquor.

From a fifth of alcohol (which, for you MOBs who don't spend a lot of time in the liquor store, is a fifth of a gallon, or about twenty-five ounces), you can serve up roughly twenty-five drinks using a one-ounce jigger to measure the liquor. Twelve bottles of liquor come in a case—using the one-ounce jigger to carefully dole out your alcohol, you can expect to serve up about 300 drinks from one case. (If you know your family likes their doubles, you'll obviously need to figure this into your equation.) One bottle of champagne or wine, meanwhile, will give you about seven drinks.

A half-keg of beer will provide the crowd with 260 eight-ounce glasses. Buying beer in a case? You'll need seven of them to equal the half-keg. And don't forget, you'll also need to stock the bar with nonalcoholic options and mixers for the liquor, not to mention lemons, limes, or anything else those drinks need for their finishing touches.

The Invitations

When looking for less expensive invitation options, you'll need to really get a handle on the process and the products. You'll want to know about paper weights (vellum? parchment? regular card stock?), about printing methods, and about all of the available options (panel cards, panel folders, overlays . . .). The Internet is loaded with discount invitation vendors; however, if your order contains the lightweight, flimsy cards when the bride *really* wanted the heavy, stiff paper . . . you'll see tears. And you'll hear the gnashing of teeth. And you'll witness the power of bridal drama at its absolute worst. It's fine to place your order with an Internet company (after you've carefully checked them out through the Better Business Bureau, of course)—just *make sure* you know what you're getting.

Chapter 9 gave you some information on the differences between printing methods. From a pricing standpoint, thermography is cheaper than engraving;

computer-printing programs are less expensive than hiring a calligrapher. Generally speaking, the more you add to invitations (more folds! more scrolls! more words!), the more expensive they're going to be. Purchasing inserts (reception cards, RSVP cards, pew cards, etc.) will also add to the final bill; while it's a nice touch to include these cards, you can absolutely print the information on the invitations and save yourself some dough.

(E) ALERT!

Research is your best bet when ordering anything online. *Thoroughly* investigate the details of invitations before you place an order. Visit some stationery stores to look through their catalogs; compare those products and services with what's available online.

The old adage "Less is more" rings true here. Your daughter can keep costs down by issuing lovely, simple invitations (not to say that plain-looking invitations are *always* the least expensive way to go—it all depends on the paper and the printing methods you've chosen). If the bride and groom (or *you*) are handy with a home printer—and have lots of time to practice—invitations can be handmade. Home printers are also an inexpensive option for printing out ceremony programs. Start early, invest in the appropriate software, and let your creative instincts take over!

Chapter 11

Wedding Day Overview

No matter how long it seems to have taken to plan this wedding, you'll wake up one day—a date you will have burned into your memory forever—and realize that *this is it*. This is the day your daughter has been waiting for; this is the day you've put so much effort into; this is the one day you've been concentrating on for the past umpteen months. What should you expect from these last minutes—and how can you ensure smooth sailing?

Prime Your Mind

It's not unusual for an MOB to feel extremely stressed on the day of her daughter's wedding; in fact, you could start feeling tense in the weeks leading up to the big day, even if you're not a high-strung person in your *real* life. What can you do to keep your cool? For starters, you need to take a realistic look at *life* before the final days and weeks prior to the wedding approach. More specifically, you need to make your own life easier during this time by not overscheduling yourself. Don't try to squeeze a vacation in two weeks before the wedding; don't agree to attend an out-of-town conference the week before; don't take on any big projects that will be due the day before the ceremony.

Ⓔ ESSENTIAL

Clear your schedule! You're going to be busy taking care of last-minute details and tying up any loose ends (and perhaps even repairing them) as the wedding draws near. You'll make yourself miserable if you take on too much too close to the wedding.

Once you've minimized your potential for overload, take a look at the outside world. Maybe it's been a while since you took the time to notice that, despite everyone's best intentions, *life isn't perfect*. You can't banish imperfection from the planet, not even for one day, not even if you plan every single detail. Don't expect the wedding day to be without its problems; in the end, you're dealing with humans (the bride, the groom, family members, vendors—all homo sapiens), and humans make mistakes, they make errors in judgment, they're emotional . . . in other words, they're flawed.

Just remember, you can greatly reduce the chance of anything going wrong by planning early and planning carefully, but you can never eliminate the potential for mishaps altogether. An MOB who can adapt and respond *calmly* to small problems is more likely to enjoy herself despite any last-minute changes in the overall wedding plans.

Pre-Wedding Preparations

Whether the ceremony is scheduled for ten in the morning or five in the evening, there will be hustling and bustling before the big event. You and the bride will want to have your hair done and your faces applied; the brides-maids will arrive with bells on (so many women in your home! so few mirrors!); and the men in your home will either skedaddle or they'll hang around trying to be helpful, until you tell them it's time to get dressed for the ceremony (and you most likely *will* have to tell them when it's time). All righty, Mom, this is it—you're *on*!

Hair Today

Depending on the length of her hair and the look she's going for, the bride may be able to do her own hair, or she may want a professional to handle the job for the ceremony. (It's advisable for most brides to leave their 'dos to someone who *won't* be a bundle of nerves on this particular day.) You'll probably want your hair done, too, so you'll either make an appointment for the same time as the bride (and perhaps the bridesmaids), or you might want to hire a stylist to come to the house. Obviously, the latter option is going to be more expensive.

Advise the bride to start working with her hairstylist at least four months before the wedding to try different hairdos. She should keep the style of her headpiece in mind, and she should take it along so the stylist can get a good idea of how the bride's hair needs to look. If the bride is going to the hair salon on the day of the wedding, she should absolutely bring her veil, and she should wear a shirt with buttons down the front, so that she won't have to smush her hair in order to dress for her wedding.

 **ALERT!**

Everyone wants to look their absolute best for the pictures, of course. Schedule hair appointments well in advance of the photographer's arrival to allow for any unforeseen, time-consuming adjustments to the bride's style (or yours or a bridesmaid's).

You should keep the appearance of your dress in mind when choosing your own hairstyle for the wedding.

If you're wearing a formal dress, have your hair *done* for the day. Nothing looks more peculiar than a head of casual hair atop a killer dress. The looks just don't gel. If you took the time to find a gorgeous gown, complete your appearance with an appropriate hairstyle.

Put on a Happy Face

Makeup is sometimes an afterthought for brides and MOBs, and understandably so. After all, most women have a day-to-day makeup routine (which may include no makeup at all) that can vary according to the time of day or a particular event—but even so, most women have been dealing with makeup for many years. They don't see the need to bring in a cosmetologist for a wedding.

Maybe you know what looks best on you. Maybe you're almost a pro yourself. Just keep in mind that you and your daughter are going to be kissing people all day long; you're going to be rushing somewhere every minute of the day; you're going to be photographed over and over and over. However, this is a very special occasion. Go ahead and treat yourself to a professional beauty workup.

Start looking for a makeup artist several months before the wedding. If you don't know of any, ask your hairdresser if she can recommend someone. It's important for you to find someone who will get a sense of who you are—you don't want to end up looking like a showgirl if you're the more conservative type (or vice versa). You can also hit the cosmetics departments in the mall for free makeovers; if you like the products, buy them. If they don't look right on you at home, go back and ask how to apply them. Don't be pressured into buying products that aren't flattering, though, or that you know you won't use.

 FACT

Working with a beauty expert is one way to make sure you'll look like a million bucks from the time you leave your home for the ceremony until you return home, worn out from the excitement of the day (but *still* looking good).

Flowers? Check!

The wedding day is a hurricane of activity: It starts first thing in the morning and doesn't end until the reception winds down. If you're not a wedding planner in your professional life (i.e., you don't deal with brides and bridesmaids and vendors on a weekly basis), you could find yourself feeling as though you've forgotten something, and not realizing what it is until you arrive in church without your corsage. One way to minimize the possibility of this happening? Make a list—and check it many, many times.

The List

Dealing with multiple vendors can be a head-spinning experience. You'll need to touch base with each of them in the weeks prior to the wedding to confirm your order. (Do this even if you've already been assured that everything will be as promised. The MOB who keeps vendors on their toes has every right to complain if things go wrong.) It's in your best interest to start assembling a list of vendors and services at least a week prior to the wedding. The list should include:

❏ *Flowers*: How many of each type (bouquets, corsages, boutonnieres, baskets for flower girls, the bride's bouquet, arrangements for the church and/or reception), and what extras (any accessories for the ring bearer, runner for the aisle), what time they should be delivered, and to which location.

❏ *Transportation*: How many limos have you hired? What color? What style? What time are they arriving? If you've hired a luxury car instead, you'll need the same information at your fingertips.

❏ *Ceremony programs*: Are they at the church, or on their way? Who's in charge of them?

❏ *The photographer and/or videographer*: When will they be arriving at the house? Any special instructions?

❏ *Musicians*: When will they set up for the ceremony? For the reception?

❏ *The cake*: What time will the bakers arrive to assemble the confection at the reception site?

❏ *Reception*: Which appetizers should be laid out for the cocktail hour? What's for dinner? You need to have a grasp on these details on the off chance that something is missing or just isn't right.

Obviously, if there's another area of concern specific to your situation (someone needs to pick Uncle Al up at the airport, for example), this should go on your list, as well. Keep a separate folder within easy reach containing contracts and phone numbers—just in case.

Help!

Now, you can make all the lists you want—you might be a champ at whipping them off, in fact—but you can't be in three places at once. You'll probably need to enlist help at some point, just to cover all of your bases. Don't try to simultaneously deal with the photographer and the florist when they both arrive at your house at the same time. Don't attempt to count baskets of flowers in the church while you're handing out ceremony programs.

Handle the larger chores yourself, but recruit a friend or a family member to help with some of the smaller tasks. Let someone else dole out the programs at the door of the church. Trust your husband to peek out the window and make sure that two black limos are in the driveway; he'll tell you if they're pink.

The photographer may want you to pose for some pictures with the bride before the ceremony, so you'll have to make sure that you're prepared when he's ready for you. Everything should be under control at that point, but you'll want to have someone on standby to help just in case phone calls need to be made, or a last-minute run to the corner store (you forgot to buy film for your camera!) is necessary.

 ALERT!

Be sure to keep an eye on the clock. If the flowers are supposed to arrive at noon, call that florist if they aren't in your home by ten past. Know when things should be happening, and do your best to keep everything—and everyone—on track.

To the Church!

To your amazement, you *will* eventually leave your home and find yourself traveling to your daughter's wedding. You may ride with her, or she may be in a separate car. If the two of you are side-by-side, try not to overload her with a lot of details. She'll probably be feeling nervous, and any last-minute instructions ("Don't forget to smile," "Make sure you aren't slouching when you're kneeling," or "Remember to speak loudly") are bound to cause her more anxiety than she can comfortably handle. Don't torment her with the specifics of the wedding, either—that's your job at this point.

Details, Details

The bride can't very well go traipsing through the church to make sure that everything is in its place prior to the ceremony, so this job will fall to you. Take a good look at the groomsmen: Are their boutonnieres on correctly? Are all of them spiffed-up and ready to go, or does *that guy* need to straighten his tie?

Take a look at the church: Have the correct flowers been delivered? Are there flowers from the last wedding that clash horribly with the baskets you've paid for? (Get rid of them, *pronto*. They'll ruin the pictures.) Have the ushers seated the guests according to their affiliations (bride's side to the left; groom's to the right), or are they weighing down one side of the church with anyone who walks through the door? (Not that you should reseat people, but you *can* instruct the ushers on how to seat guests.)

ⓔ ESSENTIAL

You can see it now: Your daughter's going to *weep* through her vows. Just in case, have one of the ushers place a package of tissues where she'll be standing for the ceremony. She can discreetly pull them out as needed.

Take a look at the bridesmaids; make sure they all have their bouquets in hand and that none have been left behind in the limo. Does the flower girl have her basket? Has she been properly instructed on where she's going, and where she will sit? If the maid of honor has a huge lipstick smear on her cheek from a well-wisher's kiss, wipe it off for her. (You want to make sure that the wedding pictures—and everyone in them—look as good as possible.) Your last duty before taking your seat is to check on the bride and to make sure she's all right. She will be, deep down, of course, but she'll want to know that you *care*, so no matter how stressed out you're feeling, *be nice*.

Calmly check these last-minute details. There's a difference between being an organized, concerned MOB and being an obsessive-compulsive control fiend. You can actually be of great help to the bride and to the attendants if you can stay in control of your own emotions; if you're rushing around, barking out orders, everyone will avoid you, and you won't be able to accomplish anything.

During the Ceremony

Once you've given the attendants the final once-over, and after you've checked on the bride, you'll be seated for the ceremony. The MOB is the last person to be escorted into the church before the march of the bridesmaids begins. If one of your sons is standing up for the groom, he might walk you to your seat; if not, you'll be seen safely to your pew by one of the ushers.

If you and the bride's dad are married to each other, you'll sit together in the front row on the left-hand side of the church (as you enter from the rear).

Unless they've been tapped by the bride to read during the ceremony or to bring up the gifts, the parents of the bride and groom usually watch the proceedings from their seats. You are not responsible for adjusting the bride's dress or veil during the ceremony, nor should you step up to grab her bouquet while the couple exchanges rings. These tasks fall to the maid of honor, and she knows what to do—so don't embarrass her by whispering loudly to her as she passes you, "Don't forget to poof the train!" Sit back and enjoy the beauty of this event, which you worked so hard to help create.

 FACT

When the ceremony ends, the bride and groom exit first, followed by their attendants, and then their parents. Don't try to sneak out before the maid of honor parades past you. Wait your turn.

The Interim

Depending on the time of the ceremony and the time the reception is set to begin, you may have several hours to fill between the two events. The bride and groom may be completely out of sight during this time, but that doesn't mean that *you* can take a break—your family and friends are all *dying* to talk to you, and you have plenty of time to spare before the reception. What should you expect to be doing during the interim, and how can you help your out-of-town guests pass the time?

Later, Gators

The entire wedding party will probably be whisked off by the photographer for scores of pictures immediately following the ceremony. Usually, this photo shoot takes about an hour, but if they're traveling to a special site, they could be gone much longer than that (and if there are several hours between the wedding and the reception, it doesn't really matter). You shouldn't expect to go with them. Sometimes the photographer will take some family photos at the ceremony site immediately following the nuptials, but usually, this time is reserved for the bridal party to show their pearly whites. You may see them before the reception, or you may not see them until you arrive at the banquet hall.

Out-of-Towners

When a wedding is scheduled for one o'clock and is being followed by an evening reception, a collective groan can sometimes be heard from the out-of-town visitors (this includes cross-country travelers as well as those who have made more than a thirty-minute drive to the ceremony). "What are we going to do to pass the time?" they wonder.

You may want to consider hosting an interim get-together at home for some of these people. Consider including the following folks:

• Guests who were nice enough to make the drive across several towns to attend the ceremony, and who don't necessarily want to spend the day driving back home and then traveling *back again* for the reception.

• Friends and family who have spent a considerable amount of time and money traveling across several states to wish the bride and groom well.

• Guests who may live nearby, but whom you see rarely.

Ⓔ ESSENTIAL

Let this be a time to catch up with your friends and family. You'll be so busy at the reception, greeting acquaintances and meeting the groom's extended family, you won't have time for a lot of good, long chats. Now's your chance.

Many guests, you will notice, will choose to skip the ceremony when there's a several-hour delay between the vows and the reception. Anyone who has cleared their entire day to attend the church service *and* the reception would like to know that you appreciate their efforts, and inviting them back to your home for a casual gathering is a great way to show your appreciation. This does not have to be a formal affair. A few deli trays and some pastries will be enough to hold over even the hungriest guests. Make sure you have enough seats for everyone, especially if the bridal party will be stopping in after the photographer has finished with them.

Keep Them Busy

If you can't host an interim party for whatever reason, make sure you've given your guests the skinny on the area: Let them know if there's something special happening in town during the wedding weekend; include points of interest, such as museums, parks, or shops. Include this information when you send their invitations. While you shouldn't try to stuff a brochure into the envelope, you might want to include some helpful Web sites along with a map of the area, highlighting any areas of intrigue.

Computer-savvy brides and grooms are finding that creating a wedding Web site is incredibly helpful for relaying pertinent information to their guests. If your daughter and her fiancé have set up their own site, ask them to send emails to friends and relatives who will be looking for some entertainment options during their stay.

The Reception

An MOB works so hard over the course of a wedding day, there should really be a great big payoff waiting for her somewhere. Wait a minute—*there is*! Your daughter's happiness and the knowledge that you were able to create a beautiful event is your reward. Not what you had in mind? There's another bonus: The reception is the time when you might finally be able to relax a little and really enjoy yourself . . . once you have approved the details, that is.

The Receiving Line

Some brides and grooms are choosing to forego the receiving line these days, complaining that it takes them away from their own party, and arguing that no guest really enjoys making their way through the never-ending lineup, anyway. Bridesmaids and ushers are forced to make small talk, and the bride and groom find themselves kissing and hugging strangers.

Your response? *Tough noogies, kids.* Anyone who comes to the wedding deserves to be personally greeted by the primary players, and there's simply no easier way to do this than by having a receiving line. Keep in mind that many of your older guests will expect this tradition, and may well feel snubbed if the bride and groom eliminate it. Imagine the response of your friends and relatives, who have made a great effort to attend this event, when they realize that the newlyweds don't want to be bothered with welcoming them—they'd rather be having *fun.* Tell the bride and groom there will be plenty of time for play once they've said hello to every single guest.

The receiving line does not have to include all of the attendants. By cutting the size of the line, you'll also cut down the time it takes for your guests to navigate it, and hence the amount of time the bride and groom will have to miss their party. The bride and groom can greet the guests by themselves, or they might want to include their parents, or only the mothers (while the fathers spend their time mingling with the guests during the cocktail hour). All of these options are perfectly acceptable.

Ⓔ ALERT!

As the structure of the traditional family is changing, the receiving line is following suit (in other words, no one is going to force bitterly divorced parents to stand next to one another and smile). Let the bride and groom choose what works best for both families.

Other Options?

There are alternatives to the receiving line, but most are fairly time-consuming and don't allow your guests the opportunity to kiss the newlyweds. One option is for the bride and groom to stop and greet the rows of guests as they leave the church. This is a good way for the bride and groom to give a quick wave and a smile to everyone in attendance. On the other hand, it's not as personal as a face-to-face greeting, and it could create a bottleneck in church. (No one wants that, especially on a hot summer day.) The bride and groom might also opt to swing by each table during dinner to say hello to their guests. This is actually a nice touch *in addition* to the receiving line, but again, it's fairly impersonal and probably not what the diehard receiving-line advocates will find acceptable.

Be On Guard!

The cocktail hour will include drinks and hors d'oeuvres, socializing, and a bevy of guests asking you where the gift table is. Most reception facilities will set up an area that's somewhat out of the way so that guests aren't constantly tripping over gifts, but it *shouldn't* be so hidden that someone could rifle through the goodies without notice. Assign a friend or relative to keep an eye on the bride's bounty.

 **QUESTION**

Is it really necessary to have someone guard the gift table?

No one *you* know would steal a present, of course, but any stranger could waltz in off the street and make off with a package or two. This is especially true of envelopes containing cash, so make sure that gift table is in plain sight and guarded.

Your official duties at the reception are to be the hostess, and to make sure everything goes according to plan. Again, there's being organized and assertive, and then there's crossing the line into being a little controlling and nutty. Nutty MOBs don't get anywhere with vendors if and when problems occur; cool-headed, well-spoken, well-informed MOBs *do*.

You and the bride will have discussed how the DJ or bandleader will introduce the wedding party. Expect to be heralded by the crowd when your name is announced. You'll take your seat and enjoy the fabulous dinner you and the bride have so carefully selected.

Order of Events

There's the cocktail hour (during which the cake will be cut), which will be followed by dinner, if you've chosen to serve a meal. Before anyone digs in, the best man traditionally offers a toast. The toasting doesn't need to stop there, though, and if your family loves to honor its members, you could find yourself listening to a long line of heartfelt speeches. If anyone would like to offer some kind words to the newlyweds, the traditional order of toasters is as follows: best man, groom's father, bride's dad, groom, bride, friends or relatives, maid of honor, groom's mother, MOB, and anyone else.

If something is amiss during dinner—the food is cold, or the service is lousy—find the banquet manager at once and make him aware of your concerns. Even if he can't fix something immediately, you need to give him the chance to rectify the situation; if he can't, you have every right to ask for a partial refund at the end of the evening. (Reputable businesses will be very apologetic if something clearly isn't right, and will refund the price of a number of dinners.) If you keep your complaints to yourself until the end of the reception, you may have far less leverage.

 FACT

> Everyone loves good leftovers! Don't be afraid—and don't feel like a cheapskate—to ask to have any uneaten dinners wrapped to take home. You've already paid for them, and they'll end up in the garbage otherwise.

Once dinner has wrapped up, the dancing will start. The bride and groom share a dance, then the bride dances with her dad, and the groom hits the dance floor with his mom. This is followed by a dance for the parents of the newlyweds, which is trailed by a song for the bride to dance with her father-in-law while you and the groom trip the light fantastic and the attendants sway in time with each other. By this time, your guests will be yawning and ready to head home, and you'll be amazed when you realize that it's after ten o'clock. *Combine some of these dances.* They're very time-consuming, for one thing; for another, you and the groom (or the bride and her new father-in-law) might feel very uncomfortable being in the spotlight by yourselves. Let the guests share the dance floor with the wedding party as soon as possible. It's in everyone's best interest.

Toss It

The bouquet and garter toss is a tradition that has been around for ages; however, it's really falling out of favor as women are starting to see it as a sexist practice. If your daughter wants to skip this all together, let her. She knows what the young women in the crowd will be comfortable with. If she fears none of them will play along with a young bachelor inching a garter up a random female leg, don't argue with her. She may still want to throw the bouquet, though, and that's perfectly fine.

Party, Party, Party

After the reception has ended, some families like to keep the party train moving. You might want to host a postwedding party, especially if the reception will be wrapping up fairly early in the evening and you know your guests will be looking to revel some more. This can be an informal, at-home affair including only a small, select number of guests, or you might want to look into keeping the party at the reception site after the newlyweds have hit the road. You can be sure that you'll end up with a larger number of guests if you choose the latter option, as there's no nice way to give anyone who's already in attendance the boot.

Chapter 12

The Best Mother-In-Law Ever

After the wedding, life goes on. (Believe it or not, it's true!) The newlyweds will be faced with piles of presents—and blank thank-you notes. They may drop out of sight or seem distant for a while. They'll also be looking for a home, and then they might realize that they haven't the slightest idea of how to take care of the place. The good MOB stands back and carefully considers what she's going to say about these issues before she says (or does) *anything*.

Sign Here

Nothing is more upsetting to a mom who has just invited legions of friends and families to a wedding than a daughter who refuses to write thank-you notes for all of the gifts that have been lavished upon her and her new husband. Is this another generation gap? Is it standard practice for brides to thank guests in person for gifts, and let it go at that? No, it isn't. This is one issue that's worth harping on until you see the bride breaking down and penning her gratitude.

Ⓔ ESSENTIAL

So, you're Mrs. Even-Steven. An MOB will sometimes look at the list of wedding gifts so that she knows what to give Aunt Ethel's daughter when she gets married. It's not a horrible idea, but just make sure your first concern isn't pettiness. A gift is a gift, after all.

It's the Right Thing

No matter what assumption the bride and groom may have been under, a guest is never obligated to either attend a wedding or to give a gift. Anyone who has bothered to bring (or send) the newlyweds a present deserves a hand-written (no fair typing up a form letter on the computer) note of appreciation. The note should be short and sincere, and should make some mention of the specific gift and its intended use.

For example, if your cousin Martha sent the bride a tablecloth, the bride could write a note along the lines of the following:

> Dear Martha,
> Thank you so much for the beautiful lace tablecloth. Jim and I just love it, and will use it for our most formal dinners. It was so kind of you to think of us.
> Love,
> Mary

If Martha has sent the ugliest tablecloth you've ever seen, the note should still read the same. (It's *really* the thought that counts.) Now, if Martha gave the newlyweds money, a thank-you note might read:

> Dear Martha,
> Thank you very much for the generous gift. Jim and I are looking for a new couch, and we'll use your money towards the purchase. It was great to see you at the wedding. I hope we'll see each other again soon.
> Love,
> Mary

Notice how there's no mention of the specific dollar amount, but the bride tells Martha exactly where that money is going to be used, which will give Martha a sense of having made a significant contribution that the kids really appreciate. In the event that the bride has no idea what Martha has given her, she can write a generic note:

> *Dear Martha,*
> *Thank you so much for the wedding gift. I was so happy you could come to the wedding and meet Jim. I hope we'll see each other over the holidays.*
> *Love,*
> *Mary*

Obviously, the writer of this note has no clue as to what the actual gift was, but the important thing is that she made the effort to thank Martha anyway. A note like this is not exactly *admirable* (and should be avoided if possible), but it's *far* worse to ignore the gift giver altogether.

No Time to Waste

If the wedding was a large one, the bride should get cracking on these notes as soon as she returns from her honeymoon. She has one month to get them out, according to etiquette. The guests will also want to know that the bride received their presents, and that nothing was lost in the shuffle.

When the bride and groom open the gifts, they should keep a list of who has given what, and refer to that list when writing their notes. (No one wants to be thanked for the wrong gift, after all.)

ⓔ QUESTION

Are thank-you notes the bride's responsibility, or should the groom help?
Of course, the groom should help out, especially if both of them are working full-time. Writing 100 or so thank-yous is a time-consuming job; two pens working furiously will cut the time in half.

Just Make Her Do It

Don't accept no for an answer here. While there are plenty of issues that are fair game for negotiation after the wedding (issues which will be covered later in this chapter), this isn't one of them. It's really *very* impolite to invite guests to a party, take their gifts, and then not acknowledge them, especially in this situation. Since some of the guests are your friends and relatives who don't know your daughter from anyone else in the world, they came to the wedding at your request. If the bride wants to leave her own friends hanging, wondering whether she liked their presents, that's one thing (because it will affect their opinion of her); however, she shouldn't be allowed to do the same to the folks you invited (because it will affect their opinion of her *and* you).

The Newlyweds' Attitude

After you've settled the issue of the thank-you notes, you'll move onto more important life issues—such as why the bride and/or groom seem to be avoiding you. It's difficult for an MOB to switch gears so quickly, to go from being so involved in the wedding to adopting a hands-off attitude with the newlyweds. Realize that the months after the wedding are a crucial time for the kids. The bride and groom *have* to establish their own sense of identity as a married couple. The relationship you establish with them here and now is going to be a foreshadowing of the years to come.

Hold Your Tongue

No one ever tells the bride and groom that learning to live together isn't always a piece of cake. The smallest problems can be worthy of award-winning dramatics from either newlywed, and brides are especially prone to telling their mothers *far* too much. Is your new son-in-law refusing to pull his weight around the house, leaving all the chores for your daughter? Is he hitting the bars with his single friends? Is he careless with money?

Obviously, any new wife would have a hard time dealing with some of these issues. It's likely that she wouldn't want to share her anxiety with a lot of people, and she doesn't trust anyone like she trusts you. This puts you in a tough spot. You're hearing the worst of it, but remember, you're not expected to pass judgment. (In fact, even if the bride *requests* judgment, keep it to yourself.)

What can you do here? Listen. If she wants advice, offer the most neutral, nonjudgmental guidance you can muster. Let her know that every newly married couple has issues to work through. Even when she's upset with him, her primary allegiance is to him. Maligning him will only cause a rift between you and your son-in-law (because somehow, somewhere, your daughter will repeat your words to him), and *that's* sure to cause trouble between you and your daughter.

(E) ALERT!

Button that lip! If the bride complains about her hubby, and *you* give a monologue cursing his character (or lack thereof), you're playing a *very* dangerous game. Chances are, the bride is going to work past her misgivings concerning her husband . . . but she won't forget how quick you were to condemn him.

Back Off a Bit

Even if you are the least judgmental mom on the planet, you can still cross the line into meddling territory if you're simply *around* too much. Remember, the newlyweds need time to get used to living together—they need to get a feel for each other's daily rhythms, habits, and quirks. They need quiet time to just sit and talk. They need to do things together, alone—things like shopping for groceries, walking hand-in-hand through the park, sitting in the laundromat together as the world passes by those huge windows . . .

 FACT

> The newlyweds haven't moved to Mars. Chances are, if you're living in the same area, they may want and *need* your assistance from time to time—with decorating, or with laying out a budget. No one is telling you that you can't see them. Just don't smother them.

They're only going to be newlyweds once, and for a relatively short time. It won't be long before they fall into the routine of many long-term marriages, where one of them is working too much, and the other one is anxious to have visitors. They'll have kids of their own soon enough, and they'll need help with the babysitting and carting the tots around town to play-dates and preschool. In other words, there will be plenty of time for you to be with them somewhere down the line. Don't crowd them in their first year of marriage, when every minute they spend together—no matter what the setting—is worthy of a romantic journal entry or an ardent poem. When they want company, they'll invite you to their home. *Avoid popping in to surprise them.*

Even if you are extremely close to your daughter, you have to give her and her new husband room to breathe after the wedding. Your exceptional relationship will very likely continue, as long as you don't put her in the awkward spot of having to avoid your phone calls and ignore your knocking at the front door so she can snag some private time with her hubby.

ⓔ **ESSENTIAL**

> Your relationship with your daughter and her husband is an ongoing work in progress. It will change from time to time, and from situation to situation. As the years go by, you'll all learn how best to deal with one another—and you'll learn which circumstances are worth your efforts.

Traditional Hotspots

So now you know to never badmouth your son-in-law (or at least not while the kids are still settling into married life), and you know you need to give your daughter and her new husband plenty of space. You should also be aware of some of the other ways well-meaning mothers-in-law get themselves into hot water with one or both of the newlyweds. Stay away from these touchy subjects:

Suggesting Upgrades to Their Home

If your daughter has always been accustomed to having the best that money can buy, it may disturb you to see her living in newlywed pauperism. They won't be broke forever, and they will resent your implying that they should be fabulously wealthy *right now*.

Talking About the Past

Your daughter was seriously considering marrying another guy (or *you* were dreaming of their union), or you feel she gave up a career for her husband. Drop it. Dwelling on what might have been is a big waste of time for you, and incredibly irritating for everyone else.

Talking About the Future

Don't push your dreams onto the newlyweds. If she and her husband are talking about starting a family, and she's going to be staying home for a few years, don't push the topic of her finishing her Ph.D. right now. (And don't push kids right away if she wants the Ph.D. first.)

Blaming the Son-in-Law

When a daughter makes a choice that is unwise (as far as her mother is concerned), it's common for Mom to look to the obvious source of the problem—her son-in-law. That's unfair. Your daughter has a mind of her own, you know.

There are countless variations of these topics, of course, and numerous other issues, as well. You're thinking that this is unfair, and that you'll either resign yourself to a life of keeping your mouth shut or you'll be criticized for everything you say to your daughter and her husband. That's not exactly true. As time goes by, you'll learn what's acceptable to them, and what isn't. But you'll also learn to care about some things, and to forget others. You may not give a darn if your son-in-law gets angry with you for encouraging your daughter to take the full-time job she's considering; on the other hand, you may decide that what your daughter and her husband do for a living doesn't really affect your life, so . . . why should you lose sleep over their decisions?

Ⓔ ALERT!

Don't criticize the groom's family. No matter how bad you or the bride might think they are, they're *still* his blood relatives. If you can't say something nice about them, try to forget they even exist.

Movin' On, and Movin' In

You know the newlywed zone is fraught with peril for the average mother-in-law. Well, then, what will you do if you're asked to help the kids find and/or settle into their new home? Surely you're allowed to let your advice flow freely, especially if your daughter and her husband (or fiancé) are doing things *wrong*. You have to tell them about the proper time to move in together (i.e., *after* the wedding), and you would just hate to see them move into a place that they won't be able to afford. (What you'd really hate more is to end up supporting them.) Wait a minute, Mom. Before you get on your little soapbox, learn how to tone down your advice to make sure you're not being judgmental on some topics.

"Don't You Dare Move in There!"

Although it's common nowadays for engaged couples to move in together before the wedding, there are still moms out there who don't approve of the setup. It's also not unheard of for a mom to condemn the move, and to give her daughter the silent treatment for bringing shame on the family name.

While this is understandable—to a point—it may be that a mother who is so viscerally opposed to the bride and groom establishing a household prior to the wedding is experiencing a culture gap firsthand.

This is the environment of the day; this is what your daughter's generation does. She's not following the crowd—she's realizing that moving in together before marriage actually has its benefits, some of which include:

• The couple is able to adjust to living with one another long before the drama and emotion surrounding a wedding affect their abilities to cohabitate.

• Wedding gifts can be sent directly to their home.

• After the honeymoon, they'll return *home*. They won't have to be concerned about packing things and moving them at an otherwise very hectic time.

• They won't be moving into a home filled with surprises after the wedding; they'll know what their monthly heating, water, and electricity bills will be.

So, although you may not be gung ho on the idea of them "shacking up," if she's already engaged to this guy, she's obviously serious about spending the rest of her life with him. What difference does it make, really, *when* they start sharing the same bathroom?

Ⓔ ALERT!

Remember, a *lot* of things were shameful years ago: A married woman working outside of the home was scandalous; women who remained unmarried were viewed as completely undesirable; divorce was unthinkable. These are common practices today, right alongside couples living together before the ink dries on the marriage license.

After the Honeymoon

Some couples still wait until after the wedding to move in together. These newlyweds are faced with finding an apartment or a house that will be available for them to move into right after the honeymoon. Of course, another option is for one of them to stay right where they are and to simply shuffle some things

around to make room for their new spouse. This is infinitely easier if it's at all possible.

However, if the bride and groom are house hunting
for a new place, they may ask you to help out or to
take a look at a certain abode and to give your opinion.
Let them know that they should really start looking for
a house as soon as they decide they're in the market
for one; an apartment usually takes less time to find,
and four months of searching should be sufficient.

 FACT

> Experts advise that a mortgage not exceed 25
> to 28 percent of a household's pretaxed
> income (though some advisors will go a *little*
> higher than this). Anything more expensive
> than that will force many couples to choose
> between heat and food.

What should they be looking for? Above all else,
they should try to find something that they can afford.
There's no better or simpler way to put it. There's
nothing more depressing (and nothing that ages young
folks faster) than being broke. Money is a huge issue in
many marriages—and in many divorces. Poverty breeds
unhappiness, which breeds resentment, which breeds
division in a relationship. If the kids are looking at a
home which is clearly out of their price range, advise

them to sit down and run the numbers *themselves*—without the "help" of a real estate agent, who is banking on her own commission.

This Goes *Here*

You've been running your own household for years. You know the most efficient way to set up a kitchen, you know which colors complement each other in the dining room, and you know how to present a work of art so that visitors feel as though they've stepped into a gallery. Your daughter, sadly, didn't inherit your gift for interior design, so you're going to have to help her out . . . *a lot.*

That's very generous, as long as she *wants* the help. If she's asking you to help her unpack in her new home, she isn't necessarily giving you permission to duplicate your floor plan on her turf. You may have suggestions, and it's fine to present them to her—but if she has ideas of her own, try to quiet your own instincts. She'll find out on her own, eventually, if her way isn't the best. Meanwhile, if you argue with her over the placement of the silverware drawer in the kitchen, she'll keep the spoons in the most inconvenient spot until she moves out, just to prove to you that she was right.

Experience Is the Best Teacher

When the newlyweds take on the responsibilities of a home and a marriage, they may slide right into their new roles without even the smallest snag. Then again, both of them may feel overwhelmed by life when they realize that they have to have food in the house and clean clothes for work, the bills have to be paid, and for some reason, none of these things *ever* get done.

 **ESSENTIAL**

> Respect your newly married daughter's space. This is her home, and she's entering the adult world now. Let her do things her way, even if it pains you to do so. Help her out with the unpacking, but don't bring in a team of your own decorators.

Years ago, home economics was a standard rite of passage for boys *and* girls (and moms didn't work outside the home, which meant that they were able to pass on certain domestic skills to their young'uns). They learned to decipher recipes and to sew buttons, if nothing else. Eventually, though, home ec faded in favor of more technical, marketable subjects, and suddenly, young men and women could graduate from high school without ever learning how to handle a mixer. What this means to you is that you may see your whiz-kid daughter and her business-savvy husband struggling with the most basic household tasks, simply because they never learned them. Can you help? As long as you know how to be handy around the home, *of course* you can.

Basic Life Boot Camp

You may feel foolish taking your daughter and her husband by the hand and teaching them how to balance a checkbook. You might feel condescending when you teach them how to fire up an iron to the appropriate material setting or when you break out the needle and thread for a crash course in button repair. You could feel ridiculous when you present the merits of using fresh food to cook with and comparing it with the high sodium and fat levels of prepared meals.

The good news is this: These are not complicated tasks, really. They should catch on to most of them fairly quickly. You won't be teaching them how to starch collars forever, nor will you need to show them how to cut an onion every time one of them plans on making a meatloaf. If only *one* of them can manage to read a recipe and learn to follow it, you'll be in the clear sooner than you think.

What's the Point?

The bad news is this: It might be difficult to impress upon either the bride or the groom the importance and *value* of knowing how to do these things. Keeping track of how much money is available in the checking and savings accounts is obviously a smart thing to do. It's almost always cheaper (and usually healthier) to whip up something at home than to swing by the fast-food place on the way home from work every night. Taking care of little clothing mishaps at home is a much less expensive option than having to rely on outside assistance for these (usually) quick fixes. *Unfortunately*, the newlyweds are living in a quick-fix generation (and *society*), where it's usually faster and easier to pay others to take care of life's mundane tasks.

Ⓔ ALERT!

If they can truly afford to toss their chores to hired help, you shouldn't be too worried about them doing it. If they're scraping pennies together to pay the rent, but for some reason, they've hired a cleaning lady . . . that's another story.

Weekend Warrior Mom

Of course, you might also be a pro at the big home projects, like plumbing repairs, wiring, and installing flooring. If your daughter is talking about remodeling, offer to teach her a thing or two about grout and tile. She'll save a bundle if she doesn't have to hire someone else.

Meanwhile, your son-in-law might want to learn how to hang wallpaper, or how to tape drywall, or countless other things that might be easy as pie for you . . . but he might feel uncomfortable asking for your help. If he musters up the courage to ask for your guidance, don't assume that he'll catch onto your home-repair lingo right away simply because he's a man. Be patient, and remember that he's *learning*. Don't revoke his tile-cutting privileges the first time he makes a mistake. Everyone has to start somewhere. You'll be helping *and* getting to know him *really* well at the same time.

Last but Not Least

Being a good mother-in-law is really an art form. It may come naturally to you, or it might take some real effort. The important thing is that you realize that all relationships are constantly evolving, and if you aren't exactly wild about your son-in-law at one point in time, you could find that six months down the road, he seems like a completely new (and improved) man.

Brides and grooms are maturing in their relationship right after the wedding—but many times, they're also struggling to mature in their *own* skins at the very same time. Technically, they're adults, but they feel like kids, and suddenly, they're coping with joint finances, in-laws, and everyday ups and downs. When your son-in-law is not exactly behaving like the Prince Charming you expected him to be, cut him a little slack. It could be that your daughter hasn't exactly been the ray of sunshine he was counting on.

It's *mostly* true that a daughter is a daughter all of her life (whereas, when sons get married, they tend to leave the nest far behind). Try to remember that she has to learn how to be a wife now, too. You can help her when she asks; just be careful not to come between her and her new husband. Let them work through the first year before you start evaluating where their relationship is headed—and where you fit into the picture.

Appendix A
Planning Timeline

Planning a large wedding takes time and organization. You'll need to know which vendors to contact and when, and you'll also need to make a little timeline for yourself to make sure that everything has been taken care of. The following timeline will give you a good overview of the whos, whats, and whens of wedding planning.

What to Do and When

Some brides opt for lengthy engagements because they know that their dream reception hall is booked solid eighteen months in advance. Other brides have less time to plan, but manage to pull off a stunning event nonetheless (with the help of the MOB, of course). Regardless of the timing of the engagement, there are some things you and the bride should get hopping on as soon as possible. Other things can wait a bit. Use the following checklist as a guideline.

As Soon as Possible

❐ Announce the engagement to the families
❐ Start narrowing down dates and times for the ceremony and reception
❐ Decide on the budget
❐ Talk about how formal or informal, and how large or small the wedding will be
❐ Divvy up the guest list numbers and draw up preliminary lists
❐ Ask friends and family for vendor recommendations
❐ Purchase and prepare (by labeling them, for example) various organization supplies
❐ Call the church; establish contact with officiant
❐ Book interviews with vendors. Start thinking about booking them if the wedding is only a year away— or earlier if you're positive *right now* that you want *this* caterer.

Nine Months Prior
- ❏ Bride should select and contact bridesmaids
- ❏ Start shopping for dresses (bride's and bridesmaids')

Six Months Prior to the Wedding
- ❏ Think about hosting an engagement party
- ❏ Finalize the guest list
- ❏ Review vendor options and finalize contracts
- ❏ Book lodging for out-of-towners
- ❏ Shop for MOB dress and notify groom's mom of style and color
- ❏ Start working with hairstylist in order to find the best *look* for the wedding. Wedding day appointments should be made.

Four Months Prior
- ❏ Order invitations
- ❏ Send engagement announcement to newspapers
- ❏ Bride and groom register for gifts
- ❏ Shower plans should be in the works
- ❏ Plan seating charts for the reception

Two Months to Six Weeks Prior
- ❏ Confirm hotel room block for out-of-town guests
- ❏ Mail invitations
- ❏ Have dress alterations made
- ❏ Bride may have her portrait taken for newspaper wedding announcement

Four Weeks Prior

- ❒ Finalize seating charts as acceptances and regrets come in
- ❒ Confirm menu choices with caterer or reception hall

One to Two Weeks Prior

- ❒ Contact guests who haven't responded to invitations
- ❒ Give final head count to the caterer
- ❒ Call and confirm dates and times with vendors
- ❒ Start making your wedding-day checklist
- ❒ Tie up any loose ends (make sure the bride has her undergarments and accessories; give your own ensemble the once-over; make sure your husband has actually been fitted for his tux)

One Day Prior

- ❒ Attend rehearsal and rehearsal dinner
- ❒ Assign last-minute duties to friends and family members
- ❒ *Get a good night's sleep*

Appendix B

What Are You *Saying?* Invitation Wording

It's time to order the invitations. Do you know what you want them to say? The following section includes options for wording even the most complicated invitations.

General Rules

In the following examples, note how almost everything is spelled out: the time, the date, the year. Very few abbreviations are permitted on formal invitations. (Mr. and Mrs. are among the few that are allowed.) Also note how the actual address of the church isn't given; the only time you would include the street number would be if the wedding were taking place in an area where leaving the address out would only create hysteria and confusion. (For example, if your daughter is getting married in a huge city, you'll probably want to let the guests know which block of a particular street the church is located on. The rules for including the street number on the invitation follow the same guidelines as writing them in a publication: Any number under 100 is written out—as in Forty-two East Avenue—anything over 100 can be numerically represented.)

The Bride's Parents Are Hosts

If the bride's parents are the sole hosts of the wedding, the invitation will read as follows:

Mr. and Mrs. Elliot Hunt
request the honour of your presence
at the marriage of their daughter
Anne Marie

to

Mr. Jacob Thomas White
on Saturday, the first of June
Two thousand and six
at one o'clock in the afternoon
Pine Ridge Methodist Church
Pine Ridge, New York

The Groom's Parents Are Hosts

Similarly, if the groom's parents are hosting, the invitation would say:

Mr. and Mrs. Andrew White
request the honour of your presence
at the marriage of
Miss Anne Marie Hunt
to their son
Mr. Jacob Thomas White . . .

Both Sets of Parents Are Hosts

If both the bride and groom's parents are helping to sponsor the wedding, the invitation should say:

Mr. and Mrs. Elliot Hunt
and
Mr. and Mrs. Andrew White
request the honour of your presence
at the marriage of
their children
Anne Marie
and
Jacob Thomas

Mixed Family Rules

When divorce and remarriage come into play, the wording is a little different.

The Mother of the Bride Is Hostess

Mrs. Elliot Hunt
requests the honour of your presence
at the marriage of her daughter . . .

This assumes the mother has not remarried and has kept her married name. If she has remarried, of course, she would use that name; if her new husband is also sponsoring the wedding, his name would be included also, but the bride would be referred to as "her" daughter (not "their"), unless the bride has been adopted by her stepfather.

Parents and Stepparents Are Hosts

In the case of divorce and remarriage all around, with all of the parents cohosting, the invitation *could* read something like this:

Mr. and Mrs. Joshua Peters
[bride's mother, remarried]
and
Mr. and Mrs. Elliot Hunt
[bride's father, remarried]

along with
Mr. and Mrs. Carl Lucia
[groom's mother, remarried]
and
Mr. and Mrs. Andrew White
[groom's dad, remarried]
request the honour of your presence
at the marriage of their children
Anne Marie Hunt
and
Jacob Thomas White . . .

Of course, in doing this, you've pushed the bride and groom way down to the bottom of the page and have made all of the remarriages the main issue instead of the wedding at hand. A better way to word an invitation like this is as follows:

Together with their parents,
Anne Marie Hunt
and
Jacob White
request the honour of your presence . . .

Bride and Groom Are Hosts

When the bride and groom host their own wedding, they would simply list their own names at the top of the invitation:

Anne Marie Hunt
and
Jacob White
request the honour of your presence
at their marriage
on Saturday, the first of June . . .

Or . . .

The honour of your presence is requested
at the marriage of
Anne Marie Hunt
and
Jacob White
on Saturday, the first of June . . .

Reception Cards

You'll also have to word the reception cards correctly. If the cards are being slipped into the wedding invitations to inform the guests of the location of the party following the ceremony, they can simply read:

Reception
at six o'clock in the evening
Pine Ridge Yacht Club
Pine Ridge, New York

The response cards would also be enclosed:

*M*_____

____ *accepts*

____ *regrets*

or more to the point:

The favour of a reply is requested
on or before the fifteenth of May
*M*_____

____ *will attend*

Index